GUATEMALA
in Pictures

Rita J. Markel

Lerner Publications Company

Contents

Lerner Publishing Group realizes that current information and statistics quickly become out of date. To extend the usefulness of the Visual Geography Series, we developed www.vgsbooks.com, a website offering links to up-to-date information, as well as in-depth material, on a wide variety of subjects. All of the websites listed on www.vgsbooks.com have been carefully selected by researchers at Lerner Publishing Group. However, Lerner Publishing Group is not responsible for the accuracy or suitability of the material on any website other than <www.lernerbooks.com>. It is recommended that students using the Internet be supervised by a parent or teacher. Links on www.vgsbooks.com will be regularly reviewed and updated as needed.

Lerner Publications Company
A division of Lerner Publishing Group
241 First Avenue North
Minneapolis, MN 55401 U.S.A.

Website address: www.lernerbooks.com

VGS

web enhanced @ www.vgsbooks.com

Library of Congress Cataloging-in-Publication Data

Markel, Rita J.
      Guatemala in pictures / by Rita J. Markel.— Rev. & expanded ed.
          p. cm. — (Visual geography series)
      Includes bibliographical references and index.
      Contents: The land—History and government—The people—Cultural life—The economy.
      ISBN: 0-8225-1998-4 (lib. bdg. : alk. paper)
      1. Guatemala. 2. Guatemala—Pictorial works. [1. Guatemala.] I. Guatemala in pictures. II. Title.
   III. Series: Visual geography series (Minneapolis, Minn.)
   F1463.M37 2004
   917.281'0022'2—dc22   2003021051

Manufactured in the United States of America
1 2 3 4 5 6 – BP – 09 08 07 06 05 04

INTRODUCTION

Because of its mild climate, deep green forests, and brilliantly colored birds and flowers, Guatemala is called the Land of Eternal Spring. But Guatemala's history—from the time the first Spanish conquistadors (conquerors) stepped ashore around 1523, through the troubled modern government—has often been more like a hard winter than an eternal spring.

More than one thousand years ago, long before the Spanish arrived to colonize the region, the native peoples were part of the great Mayan empire. The ancient Mayan civilization, centered in Guatemala, had a rich cultural and religious tradition, full of glorious ceremonies and rites. The Maya built structures of epic proportions, performed complex mathematical and astronomical calculations, and left behind books and monuments that recorded their history and beliefs. Evidence of their culture remains in the ruins of their pyramids, elaborate temples, and cities, especially in the jungles of Guatemala's Petén region.

Nevertheless, it was the Spanish who formed modern Guatemala. Looking for silver and gold, the Spanish conquistadors quickly defeated the Maya and other native peoples—often called Indians—in Guatemala. Although the indigenous (native) Guatemalans were greater than the Spanish in number, they were unprepared for the force of a European invasion. And while the Spanish did not find the precious metals they were looking for, they stayed on in Guatemala. Using the labor of the native peoples, the colonists established large plantations and were soon exporting valuable goods such as cacao (the source of chocolate) and cotton to Europe.

The Spanish set up a central government in the colony, but the system gave the Maya few rights. The native peoples became more and more isolated, while the Spanish ruling class held most of the region's wealth and power. However, this isolation did help to keep Mayan culture alive. In rural villages, many people continued to use the languages, dress, religion, and customs of their ancestors, despite

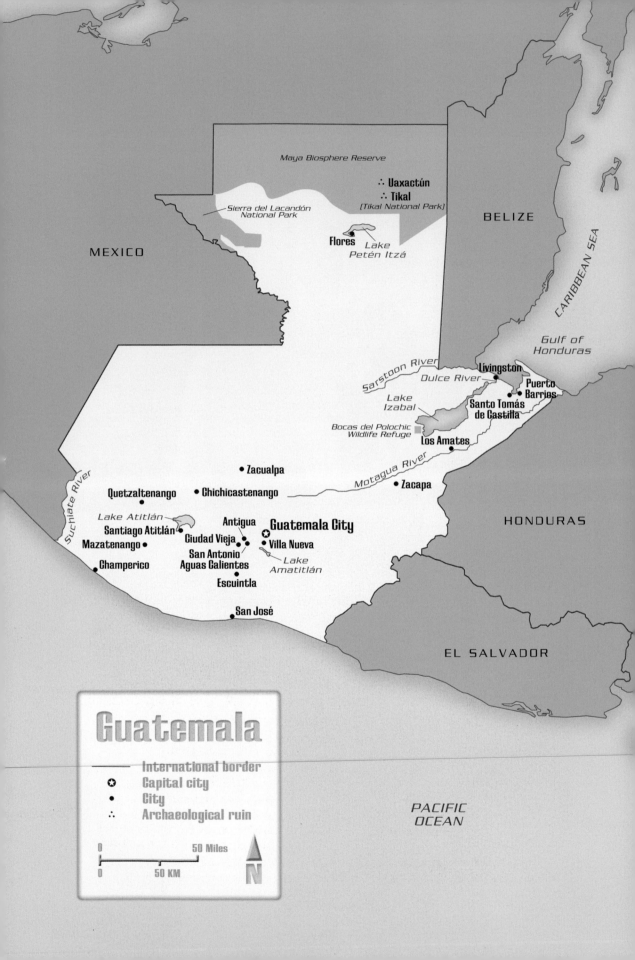

MEXICO

Maya Biosphere Reserve

∴ Uaxactún

∴ Tikal
[Tikal National Park]

BELIZE

Sierra del Lacandón
National Park

Flores
Lake
Petén Itzá

CARIBBEAN SEA

Gulf of
Honduras

Sarstoon River

Dulce River

Livingston

Puerto
Barrios

Lake
Izabal

Santo Tomás
de Castilla

Bocas del Polochic
Wildlife Refuge

Los Amates

Motagua River

• Zacualpa

Suchiate River

Quetzaltenango

• Chichicastenango

• Zacapa

HONDURAS

Lake Atitlán

Antigua

Guatemala City

Santiago Atitlán

Ciudad Vieja

☆ • Villa Nueva

Mazatenango •

San Antonio
Aguas Calientes

Lake
Amatitlán

Champerico

Escuintla

San José

EL SALVADOR

PACIFIC
OCEAN

Guatemala

— International border
☆ Capital city
• City
∴ Archaeological ruin

0 ———— 50 Miles
0 ———— 50 KM

N

the introduction of the Spanish language, the religion of Catholicism, and other Spanish influences.

Guatemala made a peaceful transition to independence from Spain in 1821. In the decades that followed, power passed from the hands of the Spanish to their Guatemalan-born descendants—often violently. A series of military leaders and forceful overthrows of the government raised tensions in the country until 1961, when civil war broke out between the government and revolutionary groups. A long and brutal conflict began that tore Guatemala apart. Numerous human rights violations took place during the war, largely against the native Maya. The war also took a terrible toll on the nation's economy, which was already vulnerable due to its heavy dependence on coffee crops.

Peace accords in 1996 ended the civil war and began a new era in Guatemalan history. The accords sought to correct many of the injustices that existed both before and during the war, and its terms guaranteed all Guatemalans the right to take part in their government. The accords also called for reforms to improve the health care, education, and civil rights of the country's poor, who make up most of the country's population and most of whom are Maya. While new challenges have emerged since the war, such as rising crime rates and increased drug smuggling through the country, peace finally gives Guatemala the potential to provide all its citizens with equal rights and opportunities. Its people also have the potential to embrace the richness of both the Mayan and the Spanish cultures.

A peace ceremony takes place every morning at the National Palace of Culture in Guatemala City. A palace guard places a fresh white rose on a sculpture of raised hands. It marks the spot where the peace accords ending the nation's civil war were signed in 1996. The previous day's rose is presented to a visitor to symbolize another day of peace in the nation. Former president Alfonso Portillo is shown taking part in the ceremony *(left)*.

THE LAND

Guatemala stretches across part of the Central American isthmus, a bridge of land that connects North and South America. With coasts on both the Pacific Ocean to the southwest and the Caribbean Sea to the northeast, Guatemala lies in the heart of Central America. The nation's longest border is with Mexico, which lies to the north and west. To the northeast is Belize, and in the southeast are Honduras and El Salvador. With an area of 42,042 square miles (108,889 square kilometers), Guatemala is only the third largest of the seven Central American countries. (The others are Belize, Honduras, El Salvador, Nicaragua, Panama, and Costa Rica.) However, with more than 12 million inhabitants, Guatemala is the most populous.

Topography

Guatemala has four major land regions, each with unique physical characteristics. These regions are the northern plain, called Petén;

the high plateau and mountain ranges, called the highlands; the Pacific coastal plain; and the Caribbean coastal lowlands.

Representing about one-third of Guatemala's landmass, Petén is the country's largest region. This limestone plateau rises to 650 feet (198 meters) above sea level in some places. It has some grasslands, but the area is primarily a dark, dense forest. Many types of forest exist in Guatemala, ranging from tropical rain forest along coastal areas to evergreen forests in the highlands. Because Guatemala's hot, humid weather is interrupted by a brief annual dry season, most of its rain forests are technically considered quasi rain forests instead of full-fledged tropical rain forests. One of Petén's most environ- mentally valuable areas of forest is the Maya Biosphere Reserve. The largest of Guatemala's protected areas, it is the center of the wildlife- rich Maya Forest, which the nation shares with Belize and Mexico. This forest is considered to be the second most important area of tropical forests still standing in the Americas.

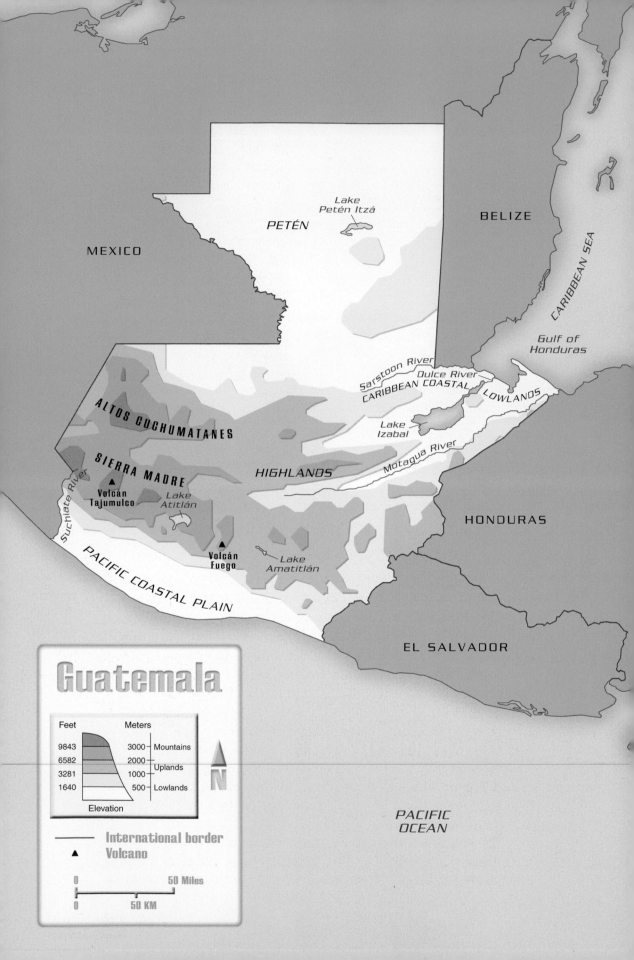

MEXICO

PETÉN

Lake
Petén Itzá

BELIZE

CARIBBEAN SEA

Sarstoon River

Dulce River

CARIBBEAN COASTAL

LOWLANDS

Gulf of
Honduras

ALTOS CUCHUMATANES

SIERRA MADRE

HIGHLANDS

Lake
Izabal

Motagua River

Suchiate River

Volcán
Tajumulco

Lake
Atitlán

HONDURAS

Volcán
Fuego

Lake
Amatitlán

PACIFIC COASTAL PLAIN

EL SALVADOR

Guatemala

Feet	Meters	
9843	3000	Mountains
6582	2000	Uplands
3281	1000	
1640	500	Lowlands

Elevation

N

International border

▲ Volcano

0   50 Miles

0   50 KM

PACIFIC
OCEAN

Petén was also once the center of ancient Mayan civilization and is the site of the best preserved Mayan ruins. However, it is the least-populated and least-developed region in present-day Guatemala. Most of its residents live in or around the area's capital, Flores, on Lake Petén Itzá.

South of Petén are the highlands, Guatemala's second-largest region. This area is filled with steep mountain ranges. It spreads across the isthmus to both of the nation's coasts. The majority of Guatemalans live here, on mountain plateaus, slopes, terraces, and in the deep valleys.

The highlands' principal mountain range, the 2,000-mile-long (3,219-km) Sierra Madre, is about 60 miles (97 km) inland from the Pacific Ocean. Running parallel to the coastline, it extends from Mexico into Guatemala and continues toward Honduras and El Salvador. To the northeast, running roughly parallel to the Sierra Madre, is the Altos Cuchumatanes mountain range, which has peaks that reach as high as 9,500 feet (2,896 m).

Many of Guatemala's western mountains are volcanoes. Some are inactive, such as Volcán Tajumulco, Central America's highest peak at 13,845 feet (4,220 m). Others are active and are carefully watched so that residents can be prepared for possible eruptions.

Volcán Fuego is probably the most threatening volcano in Central America, as suggested by its name—*fuego* means "fire" in Spanish. Records on its activity have been kept since 1524. Located only about 25 miles (40 km) southwest of the capital, Guatemala City, it has erupted more than sixty times. These eruptions have spread ash over Guatemala City and other nearby populated areas, including the cities of Escuintla and Antigua. In a major eruption, Fuego produces avalanches of volcanic matter that pour down the slope from the highlands to Guatemala's Pacific coastal plain. The geological turmoil that causes Guatemala's volcanoes also causes periodic earthquakes that have been especially devastating to the highlands, where the population is most concentrated.

Guatemala's two remaining regions are quite small. The Pacific coastal plain is a narrow strip of land stretching 160 miles (257 km) along the Pacific Ocean, between Guatemala's borders with Mexico and

Most of the world's earthquakes and volcanic eruptions occur in a beltlike pattern that loops partly around the Pacific Ocean. Scientists call this pattern the **Ring of Fire**. Guatemala's Pacific coast is part of this dangerous area.

El Salvador. With major ports at San José and Champerico, the Pacific coastal plain reaches only about 30 miles (48 km) inland, gradually sloping up to the highlands. However, despite its small size, this tropical region provides the country's best farmland. Sugar, rice, cotton, and tropical fruit grow in soil enriched by volcanic matter. Coffee grows on the cooler upper slopes of the mountains overlooking the coastal plain.

The other small coastal region is the Caribbean coastal lowlands, sometimes called the Oriente. Three river valleys stretch between the lowlands and Guatemala's interior, separated from one another by mountains. This hot, humid area extends along 100 miles (161 km) of coast and is home to the important Caribbean ports of Santo Tomás de Castilla and Puerto Barrios. These ports offer easy access to the Gulf of Honduras and the Caribbean Sea. Cargo ships and other vessels travel frequently between here and ports in the United States, South America, and Europe.

◉ Lakes and Rivers

Guatemala is home to many lakes. The country's largest, Lake Izabal, is located in the Caribbean lowlands and covers 228 square miles (591 sq. km). The smaller Lake Atitlán, in the highlands west of Guatemala City, is thought by many to be the most beautiful lake in the world. At the base of three volcanoes, Atitlán has an area of 176 square miles (456 sq. km) and is 990 feet (302 m) deep in spots.

Other important lakes include Petén Itzá, the largest lake in the Petén region. Formed when water collected in a depression in the limestone plateau, it covers an area of 40 square miles (104 sq. km). Lake Amatitlán, located 18 miles (29 km) south of the capital, is another of Guatemala's major lakes. Its steamy waters are fed by underground hot springs and believed to have medicinal powers.

Rivers also provide water for Guatemala. Several flow from the highlands toward the Pacific, providing the Pacific plain with a good source of freshwater. Most of these rivers cannot be navigated, however, as they are short and drop steep distances in the mountains of the interior. One exception is the Suchiate, some 38 miles (61 km) of which can be navigated by small boats, making it one of only three navigable Pacific coastal rivers in Guatemala.

Other rivers originate in the highlands and flow toward the Caribbean Sea. The longest of these is the Motagua, which originates near the mountain village of Chichicastenango and flows 250 miles (402 km) to the Caribbean. It is navigable for 100 miles (161 km). The Motagua flows into the Carribean along the boundary between Guatemala and Honduras. Its valley also provides the route of a major railway and highway which run alongside the river from Guatemala

Cacti grow beside the Motagua River.

City to the Caribbean. The Dulce River, navigable for its entire length of 24 miles (39 km), extends from Lake Izabal to the Caribbean. Another important river that empties into the Caribbean is the Sarstoon, forming Guatemala's border with Belize.

Climate

Guatemala's southernmost point lies in the tropics, or the region between the Tropic of Cancer and the Tropic of Capricorn. While the tropics are generally hot and humid, Guatemala's range in altitude greatly affects local temperatures. Only the coastal regions and the Petén lowlands have truly tropical temperatures, with year-round averages above 80°F (27°C). In contrast, at highland altitudes of 3,000 to 8,000 feet (914 to 2,438 m), where most Guatemalans live, temperatures average a comfortable year-round 68°F (20°C). Highland elevations above 6,000 feet (1,829 m) can freeze during the winter.

During its rainy season, Petén has lots of lakes, ponds, and streams. But during the region's short dry season, much of the water is absorbed into underwater caverns and streams, making farming difficult.

During the **eight-month rainy season,** raincoats and busy automobile windshield wipers are common sights on the cobbled streets of Antigua.

Another tropical characteristic is rain, and Guatemala has a wet climate overall. Most of the country has a rainy season lasting from May to December. But rainfall, like temperature, varies widely. Petén receives 60 to 100 inches (152 to 254 centimeters) of rain annually, compared to about 52 inches (132 cm) a year in the highlands. The Pacific coastal area tends to be the driest, receiving only 30 to 60 inches (76 to 152 cm) annually, while the Caribbean coast can get as much as 200 inches (508 cm) in one year. The Caribbean coast is also subject to hurricanes, violent windstorms that sweep in over the sea.

Flora and Fauna

A rich variety of plant and animal life thrives in Guatemala's diverse environment, with new species still being discovered. An estimated eight thousand types of plants are found here, varying with altitude and climate, and some of the country's six hundred species of orchids grow nowhere else in the world. The endangered white nun orchid— so named because the blossom's outline looks like a nun in traditional robes—is Guatemala's national flower. In addition, many native plants have valuable uses as ingredients in medicines or as building materials. Types of trees include palm, pine, oak, and mahogany.

The ocelot, found in the forests and grassy plains of Guatemala, is about twice the size of a big house cat.

A wide variety of animals—such as monkeys, jaguars, ocelots, armadillos, tapirs (a hoofed, nocturnal animal with a long snout), bears, crocodiles, spiders, and mosquitoes—roam Guatemala. The nation is also home to some of the world's deadliest snakes, including the *barba amarilla*, or fer-de-lance, the boa constrictor, and the pit viper. Birds—some of them very rare—range from colorful macaws to robins and wrens.

Watch out for the barba amarilla if you go hiking in Guatemala's forests. These snakes are some of the world's most venomous and most aggressive, and their bite can be fatal to animals and humans.

◉ Natural Resources

Extremely fertile soil is one of Guatemala's most valuable resources. However, because of the mountainous terrain and thick vegetation, only about 12 percent of the land can be farmed. Other natural resources include mineral deposits of antimony, lead, nickel, zinc, copper, and small amounts of cadmium and silver. The nation's forests provide valuable gums, oils, drugs, and dyes, as well as wood.

Guatemala also has oil reserves, concentrated in Petén, as well as small known natural gas reserves and the possibility that more may be found. Geothermal power, which is drawn from heat inside the earth, is another potential energy source. However, more than 90 percent of the country's power comes from hydroelectric plants, which get their energy from water sources. These facilities are cheap and environmentally safe to run, but they can be vulnerable to weather and natural disasters.

○ Environmental Issues

Guatemala has ecological concerns as its growing population increases demands on the environment. Deforestation is a major problem, with more than 200,000 acres (80,940 hectares) of forests, including rain forest, being lost every year. Soil erosion, in which topsoil is lost to flooding and landslides, is also a serious issue, and water pollution is increasing.

Tree harvesting and oil exploration in the Petén region have put Guatemala's environment at further risk. Guatemala has created groups and laws to protect its environment and endangered species. Local individuals and groups, often supported by international organizations such as the World Rainforest Movement, have tried to publicize violations and to block development that they consider harmful to the environment. Areas such as the Sierra del Lacandón National Park, the Bocas del Polochic Wildlife Refuge, and the Maya Biosphere Reserve are protected from development.

A special protected area within the Maya Biosphere Reserve is the Mario Dary Rivera Biotope (locally known as Biotopo del Quetzal), near the ancient Mayan ruins at Tikal. The biotope's most famous inhabitant is the quetzal, Guatemala's brilliantly colored national bird. Due to deforestation and poaching (illegal hunting), the quetzal is endangered. The Mario Dary area is also home to other birds, including toucans, as well as exotic plants and trees.

○ Cities

About 40 percent of Guatemalans—nearly 5 million people—live in urban areas. The vast majority of these city dwellers live in and around the nation's capital, Guatemala City. The capital has an estimated population of more than 1 million people, and the sprawling areas around the city may have another 2 or 3 million residents. Other Guatemalan cities of historical and cultural importance are Quetzaltenango, Antigua, Chichicastenango, and Flores.

Spectacular coloring and long tail feathers make the **male quetzal** stand out in the forests of Guatemala.

GUATEMALA CITY The capital of Guatemala since 1776, Guatemala City is located on a plateau in the south-central part of the country. Like much of Guatemala, the capital faces natural dangers. In fact, Guatemala City had to be almost totally rebuilt following a series of quakes in 1917 and 1918, in which some 30,000 people lost their lives.

Despite its risky location, Guatemala City remains the country's center of industry, finance, and government. It is built on a grid pattern, with streets running east to west and avenues north to south, but rapid, unplanned growth has disrupted the order and strained the city's resources. The result is crowding, pollution, water and power shortages, and too little public transportation.

Visit vgsbooks.com, where you'll find links to more information about Guatemala's cities—including what there is to see and do, the climate and weather, population statistics, and more.

The more modern sections of **Guatemala City** are called New City. Its clubs and restaurants stay open late, and its museums and cultural sites draw wealthy crowds.

The contrast between the rich and poor is sharp in Guatemala City, where wealthy areas are sometimes surrounded by jumbles of makeshift dwellings that house the very poor.

OTHER CITIES Called Xela by locals, Quetzaltenango is Guatemala's second largest city, with a population of about 150,000. Commerce in Xela began in the nineteenth century, when the city was a major center for the coffee trade. In modern times, many tourists use Xela as a base for day trips to highland Mayan villages such as Chichicastenango.

Antigua, a former capital, retains the beauty of its Spanish colonial architecture. Even after volcanic eruptions, earthquakes, floods, and fires, the city's residents are proud of its status as a national cultural site. Only about one hour by bus from Guatemala City, it seems much farther away from the larger city's noise and chaos. Antigua is surrounded by coffee plantations, orange groves, and macadamia-nut farms. The city's 30,000 or so residents include artists, merchants, businesspeople, and more.

Another important Guatemalan city is Chichicastenango. Called Chichi for short, it is a living center of Mayan culture. Despite its population of fewer than 15,000 inhabitants and its relative isolation in the highlands northwest of Guatemala City, this ancient town is one of Guatemala's most important trading spots. Local farmers and craftspeople come here to sell their produce and goods, including traditional needlework and other forms of folk art. Many of them carry on their business dressed in the same colorful costumes that their ancestors wore. Chichi is also a place where Maya come to celebrate their own blend of traditional and Christian worship and celebration.

Flores, the capital city of Petén, has a population of about 2,000 to 3,000 people and is rich in history and natural beauty. This picturesque town, with winding cobblestone streets, is built on an island in Lake Petén Itzá. Flores is also thought to be one of the first Mayan cities visited by the Spanish and possibly the last to be conquered. Because its residents fled into the jungles when the Spanish came, it became known as a "lost" city of the Maya.

In Chichicastenango, performers stage the colorful, traditional **Dance of the Spanish Conquest** for holidays throughout the year. They dress as Mayans *(above)* and conquistadors *(left)*.

HISTORY AND GOVERNMENT

Centuries before European explorers journeyed to the Americas, farmers settled on the fertile soil of Guatemala. Archaeologists have found evidence of settlers as early as the 1000s B.C. By about A.D. 250, these native people, called the Maya, had developed an advanced civilization. Guatemala's Petén region was the center of their culture, and Mayan groups were also spread out over approximately 210,000 square miles (543,900 sq. km) of land across Central America.

The Maya

The years between A.D. 250 and 900 are known as the Classic Period of Mayan history, during which the culture was at its height. Historians think that, like in ancient Greece, Mayan society was organized into powerful city-states that controlled not only their own people but those in the surrounding countryside and smaller cities. Important cities such as Tikal had populations of more than

100,000 people. However, there is no evidence that these cities were ever united under a single government. Instead, local political and religious leaders may have ruled the Maya. These rulers were the most powerful members of society, followed by other wealthy and noble Maya, farmers, craftspeople, and slaves.

Mayan society was primarily agricultural, growing crops including maize (corn), beans, squash, and chili peppers. Some Maya farmed in villages and rural areas. Others lived in thatch-roofed homes around the city centers and farmed fields in outlying areas.

Religion was a very important part of everyday Mayan life. People prayed, fasted, and made animal and human sacrifices to their many gods and goddesses. Ceremonies were held at the major cities, in open plazas bordered by pyramids, temples, and monuments. The Maya transported, carved, and laid the stone for these enormous structures without the use of iron tools, the wheel, or pack animals.

In addition to their architectural feats, the Maya were the first people in the Western Hemisphere known to have developed a written language. Like ancient Egyptian writing, it was based on glyphs, symbols that represent sounds, objects, or ideas. To honor the gods and to record important historical events, the Maya carved and painted glyphs on monuments, temples, and other structures. The Mayan language was also set down in books called codices. Written mostly on tree bark, the codices recorded rulers, wars, astronomy, agriculture, and mythology. However, only a few of these books remain. Many were destroyed by the Spanish conquerors, while others simply deteriorated over time. Language experts still study the remaining codices and the ruins of Mayan cities, trying to interpret the glyphs.

Ancient Guatemalan languages were related to each other but varied from place to place. The spoken Mayan of the highland areas, for example, was considerably different from that of the lowland areas. Although uncertainty exists regarding the exact number of Mayan languages, experts at Guatemala's Academy of Mayan Languages have officially agreed on twenty-two. These ancient languages, including Quiché (also spelled K'iché), Cakchiquel, Kekchi, and Garífuna, are still spoken by Indian groups throughout the country.

The Maya were also advanced in math and science. By A.D. 300, they had developed a mathematical system, based on the number twenty. The Maya represented numbers with different arrangements of dots and dashes, and their system included a seashell-like symbol for zero. No other culture is known for certain to have used the zero before this time. The Maya used their mathematical skills to study the skies. Without the use of telescopes, their astronomers made careful observations and calculations to measure distances in the sky and on the ground. The Maya could also predict events such as eclipses, and used their observations to measure time and to develop a calendar that guided agricultural cycles and religious festivals. This calendar differs from the modern calendar by only a matter of seconds.

Around A.D. 900, the Maya began to leave the southern areas of their territory, including Petén and its cities of Tikal and Uaxactún. No one knows exactly what caused the Mayan migration, which ended the greatest period of their civilization. Some believe it was a sudden natural disaster or an outbreak of disease. Others think that the farmers simply wore out the soil and other resources and went in search of better conditions.

The Maya moved to what became northern Guatemala and into the Yucatán Peninsula, which stretches northward into Mexico and Belize and northeastward into the Caribbean Sea. Groups such as the Toltecs rose to power. Internal conflict grew, eventually dividing the native people into warring factions. While the Maya fought each other, Spanish conquistadors established control over the land and over the Maya.

◉ Spanish Conquest

Christopher Columbus is thought to be the first European to encounter the Maya near the area that became Guatemala. His son wrote that in 1502 Columbus's men met a group of native people paddling a large canoe full of trading goods such as cacao beans, copper, tools, and brightly colored cloth. Other explorers for Spain soon came to the Americas as well. Many of them arrived with the goal of converting the native people to Catholicism, a branch of Christianity that was Spain's official religion at the time. However, they also sought to conquer and colonize the region for Spain. By 1524 the Spanish controlled Mexico and most of Central America. First the great Aztec civilization of Mexico and then the Maya fell in campaigns led by Spanish conquistadors such as Hernán Cortés and his lieutenant Pedro de Alvarado.

Although the indigenous people fought the conquistadors, the Spanish had the advantage of horses, metal armor, guns, cannons, and other weapons. Spanish military leaders also recruited members of warring native groups and used them against each other. However, the

After conquering Guatemala in 1524, **Pedro de Alvarado** became the first governor of the Spanish province.

European diseases that the Spanish carried with them proved to be the deadliest force of all. Never before exposed to these illnesses, which included measles, smallpox, and influenza, the native peoples of the Americas fell ill and died in huge numbers. By the end of the sixteenth century, an estimated 70 to 90 percent of the Maya had died from disease or battle.

Colonial Life

The Spanish established their first Guatemalan capital, Santiago de los Caballeros, in 1524, but by 1543 they had built a new capital called Antigua. From Antigua, they ruled the colony using a form of government called a captaincy general. Under this system, the land was divided into provinces, consisting of present-day Guatemala, part of Mexico, Honduras, El Salvador, Nicaragua, and Costa Rica. Within these provinces, mayors and local councils governed villages and towns. Governors were appointed to individual provinces, and the captain-general himself lived in the capital to oversee the governors. At the very top of the colonial government was the Real Audiencia, or Royal Court, which reported directly to the king of Spain.

But Spain's captaincy general in Guatemala was not always well administered, causing deep divisions in Guatemalan society. Families of the Spanish nobility ruled the colony, competing with one another

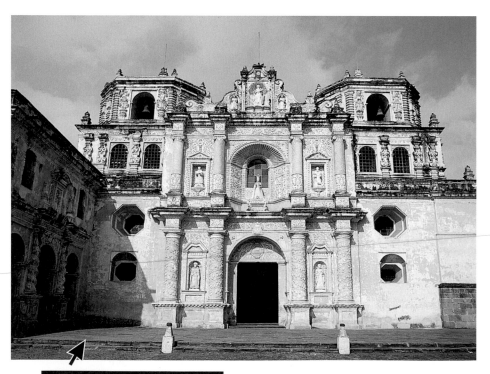

La Merced, a church in Antigua, was originally built in the mid-1500s, though the church later had to be reconstructed after an earthquake.

for power and wealth. Positions in the captaincy general were often sold or given to relatives of the king and other nobles, rather than filled by experienced or qualified administrators. These officials and their families usually led lives of comfort and wealth.

As generations passed, many people of Spanish blood were born in Guatemala. Many of them became wealthy plantation owners, traders, and merchants. Their descendants, together with those of the Spanish nobility, controlled most of Guatemala's wealth and power. Further down the social ladder were mestizos, Guatemalans of Spanish and Indian descent. At the bottom were the Maya and other Indians.

Spain grew rich from its Central American colonies, securing its position as the world's greatest sea power. Although the conquistadors had come to the region looking mainly for gold and silver, these resources proved to be disappointingly small. Looking for other ways to profit, the colonists began exporting various goods from the new colonies to Europe. But along with these exports came trade regulations and taxes. For example, colonists could not export goods that competed with Spanish products, such as wine and olive oil. Heavy taxes were imposed on Guatemala's noncompeting exports, such as cacao, indigo (blue dye), and cotton.

The Spanish were not alone in gathering riches from the Americas. Pirates of the Caribbean Sea were eager to attack Spanish ships laden with valuable goods. At the same time, Spain's high export taxes and tough trade policies encouraged a lively business in smuggled goods. During the 1700s, British seafaring traders readily accepted any illegal items that Guatemalan merchants and growers managed to get past the colonial officials without detection.

In response to grumbling from colonial planters and merchants, who wanted greater profits, Spain put forth laws to prevent unrest among its wealthiest colonists. However, some of these measures were hard on the Maya and other indigenous groups. For example, a policy of *reducciones* forced native people to resettle in small highland villages. Officials assured the Indians that this arrangement would protect them, since non-Indians would not be allowed to live with them. But the system also made it easier for some colonists to control the local population and to take control of their lands. Another policy, called the *encomienda*, allowed plantation owners to force the native people to work for them, leaving the Maya little time to farm their own land.

Many Catholic groups founded institutions such as schools in Guatemala. In 1694 **Francis of St. Joseph,** a Franciscan, founded a college in Guatemala.

The Spanish also continued their efforts to convert the native people to Catholicism. Groups within the Catholic Church, such as the Jesuits, Dominicans, and Franciscans, established themselves throughout Guatemala and Central America. Some priests dedicated themselves to working for the benefit of the native people, and some Maya gained entry to schools and hospitals set up by the various religious orders. But the orders themselves often saw great profit as well. Acquiring vast tracts of land and sometimes using native labor, they accumulated great wealth and power in Guatemala.

Independence

In the late 1500s, Spain's position as the world's greatest power began to slip. Poor administration, big spending, and a series of wars gradually weakened the empire. The biggest blow came in 1588, when Spain sent the Armada, its great fleet of ships, to attack Great Britain. The two nations were in an ongoing conflict over religious differences and colonial power. The battle was a disaster for Spain. Of the Armada's original 130 ships, only about half of them returned home—and many of those were badly damaged. The others were either sunk by the British navy or destroyed by stormy weather in the North Atlantic Ocean.

Spain's weakness caused many of its territories to revolt during the 1600s and 1700s. Although the encomienda system officially ended in 1720, discontent still simmered in Central America. The transatlantic slave trade began in the late 1700s, as plantation owners looked for more workers. Although the trade brought relatively few African slaves to Guatemala compared to countries in North and South America, some slaves did arrive. As they joined the local population, their dissatisfaction added to the general unrest.

Two major revolutions—in the United States in 1776 and in France in 1789—inspired Guatemalans to seek their independence too. Then, in the early 1800s, Spain became entangled in a costly war against the French emperor Napoleon Bonaparte. Recognizing that Spain was no longer able to control Guatemala, Spanish captain general Gabino Gaínza signed the Act of Independence in 1821. Other Central American states soon followed suit and established their own independence. By 1824 present-day Guatemala, Nicaragua, Costa Rica, El Salvador, and Honduras had formed the United Provinces of Central America.

This loose union of states wrote a constitution similar to that of the United States, specifying civil rights for individuals. Leaders such as Francisco Morazán and Mariano Gálvez oversaw the building of schools and roads throughout Central America, and new laws got rid of the death penalty and gave citizens the right to be tried by a jury.

Struggle for Change

While the United Provinces made many changes, the region's wealthy ruling classes and landowners—often called conservatives—remained powerful. They strongly opposed liberals, who wanted more drastic reforms. Largely because of this conflict, the union of states was officially dissolved in 1838. One year later, Guatemala officially declared itself an independent nation and Rafael Carrera seized power. Carrera went on to become Guatemala's dictator, electing himself president for life after fourteen years in power. With the support of conservative church officials, Spanish nobility, and wealthy landowners, Carrera cancelled many of the United Provinces' expansions of civil rights, especially for native peoples.

Carrera was followed by Vicente Cerna, another conservative. Cerna's harsh policies sparked a series of uprisings. The unrest brought

THE NAME GAME

Most Guatemalans have two last names—the father's followed by the mother's. However, most of the time they only use one of these names. For example, the full name of the man who was the dictator in Guatemala from 1898 to 1920 is Manuel Estrada Cabrera *(below)*. He would generally go by the name Manuel Estrada, using his father's family name. Occasionally, if the mother's family name is more impressive or well known than the father's, a man might use her family name instead. When a woman marries, she usually drops her mother's name and uses her father's name followed by her husband's, linked with the word "de." For example, Ana Cerano Velásquez might become Ana Cerano de Cruz. A person's name is alphabetized according to which last name he or she usually uses.

liberal reformers to power, such as Miguel García Granados in 1871 and Justo Rufino Barrios in 1873. Under their administrations, the privileges of the wealthy and the church were suspended again, and other reforms were made in government, education, and religion. But discontent was still high. After President José María Reina Barrios was assassinated in 1898, Manuel Estrada Cabrera came to office and would hold power for twenty-two years.

Under Estrada's rule, the government encouraged foreign businesses to set up in Guatemala, attracting them with tax cuts, cheap land, and cheap Mayan labor. The largest of these companies was the United Fruit Company. Based in Boston, Massachusetts, the company developed huge banana plantations in Central America. Coffee also became a thriving export business. Foreign interests and influence in Guatemala grew. However, the native people did not directly benefit from any of the reforms. Voting rights were given only to a small number of non-Mayan male landowners, and both liberals and conservatives largely ignored Mayan interests. In addition, most non-Indian Guatemalans discriminated against the Maya, believing that they were inferior to them. In response to the situation, the Maya sometimes raised rebellions that were then put down by government forces.

Meanwhile, the power and influence of foreign companies continued to grow in the early 1900s. At the same time, opposition to these companies—which held huge tracts of Guatemalan land—also grew. When Jorge Ubico Castañeda was elected in 1931, he fed this unrest by granting more privileges to foreign investors and continuing to supply them with cheap native labor. His measures were widely unpopular, but they did manage to save the country from economic disaster during a period of worldwide financial crisis.

Nevertheless, Ubico's views would eventually destroy him politically. Ubico was a follower of fascism, a political theory that believed in a powerful government and had little regard for individual freedom. In 1944 a group of civilians (nonmilitary personnel) and soldiers staged the October Revolution, forcing Ubico to resign. At the time, he was one of Guatemala's wealthiest landowners.

Under Ubico's rule, the Maya were required to work at government jobs or on the plantations of the wealthy for a minimum of 100 to 150 days per year. If they could not prove that they had fulfilled this policy, they were either put in jail or physically punished.

Ten Years of Spring

After the October Revolution, a three-man military junta (ruling council) held power until a new constitution was written and elections were held. The liberal Juan José Arévalo Bermejo was elected president and almost immediately began making moderate reforms. He gave all men the right to vote, along with literate women—although most Guatemalan women could not read, regardless of their social class. Arévalo improved health systems by building clinics in poor rural areas, providing safe water, and establishing sewage systems, which greatly decreased the risk of common diseases such as cholera. In addition to health reforms, he made education more available to the poor, increased the power of labor unions (organizations of workers to help workers), passed laws to restrict child labor, and established a minimum wage.

These changes were a great help to the poor, including the Maya. The only major issue that Arévalo did not address was land reform. That challenge was left to his successor, Jacobo Arbenz Guzmán. Elected in 1950, Arbenz tried to reduce the control of foreign companies over Guatemala's economy. He also worked to return land to the native people. Under the 1952 Law of Agrarian

Reform, the government reclaimed unused land from wealthy Guatemalans, the Catholic Church, and foreign companies. This land was given to the poor, who then had to pay the government a percentage of any profits they made. But opposition to Arbenz's land reform was intense, especially from the international companies that owned huge areas of valuable land. Arbenz's requirement that landowners pay overdue taxes was also highly unpopular.

One supporter of some of Arbenz's actions, especially his land reforms, was a political group called the Communists. At that time, the United States viewed Communism as a serious threat to national safety. Arbenz himself was not a declared Communist, but his government gave freedom to all political parties—including Communists. This policy helped convince the Central Intelligence Agency (CIA) and U.S. president Dwight D. Eisenhower to take action in Guatemala. In 1954 the CIA supported a military coup (sudden overthrow), known as Operation Success, that forced Arbenz out of office.

The coup placed Carlos Castillo Armas in power. A new constitution was written, the Law of Agrarian Reform was undone, and land was taken back from the poor. Voting rights were again restricted to the literate male minority. All reformist political groups with Socialist or Communist beliefs were outlawed. Labor leaders and other reformers were executed without trial. The Maya saw their rights shrink again. And a decade of reform—known as the Ten Years of Spring—was overturned.

COLD SHOULDER

The 1954 Guatemalan coup occurred during the Cold War between the world's two superpowers, the United States and the Union of Soviet Socialist Republics (USSR). Lasting from the late 1940s until around 1990, it was a long, chilly standoff instead of a "hot," or fighting war.

During the Cold War, Communist and non-Communist forces struggled to gain power and influence throughout the world. Afraid that Communist nations might work together to overtake and destroy non-Communist countries, the United States and other non-Communist countries tried to discourage Communist influence. Nevertheless, Communist ideas were becoming increasingly appealing to people whose governments and economies were controlled by small, elite groups of citizens.

People in Villa Nueva view photos of local victims of violence on a government office building wall. In the days following President Arbenz's overthrow, his loyal police officers formed a rebel army and killed many people whom they suspected of being anti-Communist.

◉ Years of Terror

Following Operation Success, Guatemalan politics once again became a struggle between conservative right-wing groups, which supported policies favoring landowners and the wealthy, and liberal left-wing groups favoring reform. The United States also became more involved in this struggle, supporting dictators who opposed Communism and supported U.S. businesses in Guatemala. In 1961 this intense political struggle finally erupted into civil war. A vicious conflict began between Guatemala's right-wing military forces and liberal guerrilla fighters, who were not officially organized into an army but who banded together in the war.

The war raged on in the 1970s and early 1980s, which were years of terror for all Guatemalans. Under the administration of the right-wing dictator Carlos Arana Osorio (1970–1974), death squads executed anyone suspected of sympathizing with the left-wing revolutionaries. Many Maya were accused of helping or joining the guerrillas, and hundreds of villages in the countryside and highlands were destroyed.

In the cities, supporters of the right-wing forces formed groups such as the Mano Blanco (White Hand) and Ojo por Ojo (Eye for an Eye). These organizations murdered Guatemalans who spoke out against the government or were suspected of having left-wing ties. Unions, rural groups to help the Maya, and liberal journalists were also targeted. At the same time, some left-wing groups kidnapped and murdered right-wing politicians and business leaders.

A disaster of a different nature struck Guatemala in 1976, when a major earthquake caused widespread damage. The quake was

The 1976 earthquake badly damaged this pharmacy in Guatemala City. As the civil war continued, it was particularly hard to lose such critical medical facilities.

especially devastating to poor areas, where housing could not withstand its force. The casualties were high, with estimates approaching thirty thousand people dead and seventy thousand injured. The homes of more than one million people were destroyed. Foreign countries, including the United States, sent aid to help the needy.

As Guatemalans struggled to recover from the earthquake, left-wing revolutionary groups such as Ejército Guerrillero de los Pobres (Guerrilla Army of the Poor) and Organización del Pueblo en Armas (Organization of the People in Arms) increased their strikes against the government. In the early 1980s, four guerrilla groups united as the Unidad Revolucionaria Nacional Guatemalteca (Guatemalan National Revolutionary Union, or URNG). The URNG's goal was to bring down the government.

The government, in turn, remained determined to wipe out the revolutionaries. Because guerrillas tended to gather in the rural highlands, government attacks aimed at the revolutionaries often targeted Mayan villages. Although very few Maya were involved with the guerrillas, many of them were killed or had their homes and land destroyed.

Meanwhile, control of the government changed hands through coups, passing from one military administration to the next. The dictator José Efraín Ríos Montt took power in 1982, and his short time in office—ending with another coup in 1983—saw a peak in the violence against the guerrillas and their sympathizers. Ríos Montt gathered Guatemalans, including Maya, to serve in a local force known as the PAC. Directed by the military, these groups attacked guerrilla soldiers and their suspected sympathizers. Participation in the PAC was officially voluntary. However, Ríos Montt was reported to have told the Maya that they would be executed unless they joined the PAC and agreed to report suspicious activity in or around their villages.

The Guatemalan government's abuses of Mayan human rights spurred the international community to take action. The United States condemned the Guatemalan government and cut off military and economic aid to the country. Frightened tourists stopped traveling there. Many Catholic priests, nuns, and missionaries began speaking out on behalf of the Maya as well, although this often placed their own lives in danger.

Human-rights groups such as Americas Watch and Amnesty International reported that by the end of 1982 as many as 200,000 Maya and other civilians had been killed in the war. Thousands of others were forced into hiding in city slums, jungles, and hills, or fled to foreign countries. Some Guatemalans, including many children, simply disappeared. In all, tens of thousands of crimes were committed against the Guatemalan people, giving the nation a reputation as one of the world's worst offenders of human rights.

An Uneasy Peace

In 1985, bowing to international pressure, Guatemala held general elections. A civilian, Marco Vinicio Cerezo Arévalo, was elected. A new constitution was written, and the congress began meeting again.

Meanwhile, outside powers tried to help Guatemala end its civil war. The first of these attempts was the 1987 Esquipulas Accords, a peace proposal signed by the presidents of Guatemala, Costa Rica, El Salvador, Honduras, and Nicaragua. Further negotiations began in 1991 between the Guatemalan government and the URNG, and a cease-fire was signed in March 1996. An official treaty, called the peace accords, was signed that same year. Among other things, the accords promised a smaller Guatemalan army, the return of guerrilla fighters to civilian life, and the recognition of native peoples' rights. After thirty-six long years of conflict, Guatemalans were experiencing a tentative but welcome peace.

The Pursuit of Justice

In 1997 the United Nations—an international organization that works to keep peace among nations—helped oversee putting the peace accords into effect. In addition, the World Bank, the Inter-American Development Bank, and foreign governments offered the war-torn country aid to rebuild.

However, President Cerezo Arévalo and the presidents who succeeded him were slow to follow through on some of the agreements of the peace accords, such as bringing human-rights violators to justice. Despite risks and obstacles, however, journalists, political activists, and lawyers continued to seek information regarding abuses committed during and after the war. In 1998 the issue gained new attention, when Bishop Juan Gerardi Conedera released a four-volume study of human-rights abuses during the civil war. Gerardi's study concluded that most of the abuses had been carried out by Guatemala's military. Shortly after the report's publication,

The United Nations Verification Mission in Guatemala (MINUGUA) concluded that, as of early 2000, the Guatemalan government had instituted 62 out of the 170 reforms it had agreed to in the 1996 peace accords.

Catholic students hold a poster of **Bishop Gerardi** *(far left on the poster)* in front of his tomb in the Metropolitan Cathedral in Guatemala City. They are attending a commemorative vigil on the third anniversary of his murder.

Gerardi was beaten to death. Three military officials and one civilian were the primary suspects for his murder.

In 2000, amid the controversy surrounding Gerardi's death, President Alfonso Antonio Portillo Cabrera took office. Portillo was elected partly on his promise to carry out the peace accords. Although he was a member of the right-wing Guatemalan Republican Front (FRG), he did appoint some left wingers and indigenous Guatemalans to his administration. He also publicly accepted the government's role in human-rights violations during the civil war and in 2001 oversaw the payment of $1.8 million to a Mayan village in compensation for 226 civilians killed by the military. Portillo's critics believe, however, that he has close political ties to Ríos Montt and that his government is unlikely to bring Ríos Montt to trial for human-rights violations during the war.

Nevertheless, in 2001 the Guatemalan courts ordered investigations of Ríos Montt and other former officials for their possible involvement in war crimes. In addition, the Gerardi case eventually came to trial, despite death threats against the prosecutors. The military officers were found guilty and sentenced to long prison terms. However, another court overturned the verdict, and as of 2003, the case was still awaiting a ruling from the Supreme Court. Meanwhile, special prosecutors continued to read eyewitness accounts of wartime murders in twenty-one indigenous villages. These testimonies are intended to be part of a suit against top military officers. But this type of progress occurred at the same time as new violations were being committed. Since the Gerardi murder trial, more than one hundred new physical attacks or acts of intimidation against human-rights activists were reported.

Maya escort the **coffins of civil war victims** to a new cemetery in Zacualpa. In the early twenty-first century, hundreds of bodies were found in more than six hundred secret mass graves from the 1980s.

> To discover more about the fascinating Mayan civilization, historical facts about Guatemala, biographies of Guatemala's leaders past and present, and government information, go to vgsbooks.com for links.

○ Government

Guatemala's democratic government is made up of three separate branches—the executive, legislative, and judicial. The nation's 1985 constitution, together with amendments made in 1993, guarantees citizens rights including freedom of speech, a free press, freedom of assembly, and freedom of religion.

The president heads the executive branch. Guatemalan presidents and vice presidents are elected by Guatemalan voters for a single four-year term. Every candidate for office is supported by a political party, such as the Guatemalan Republican Front (FRG), National Advancement Party (PAN), New Nation Alliance (ANN), and Unionists (Unionistas).

The president appoints a cabinet of advisers on different government issues, such as the economy. The president also selects a governor for each of the country's twenty-two subdivisions, called departments.

The legislative branch is made up of a congress of 113 members. Like the president, congresspeople are elected by voters and serve a single term of four years. Members of the congress, in turn, elect the thirteen judges of the Supreme Court, which is the highest court in the judicial branch. Important criminal and civil cases go to the Supreme Court, while constitutional matters are handled by the Constitutional Court. At the local level, residents elect mayors and city councils.

THE PEOPLE

With about 12.4 million people, Guatemala has the largest population in Central America. Its population density is estimated at 294 people per square mile (114 per sq. km). In other words, if Guatemala's population were evenly spread across the country, every square mile would be home to approximately 294 people. But since the population is spread out very unevenly across the country, parts of Guatemala are extremely crowded. The highland areas, which have the best climate, also have the highest population. On the other hand, Petén, which is mostly jungle and has a tropical climate, has the lowest population.

Meanwhile, Guatemala's population continues to grow. At its estimated annual growth rate of 2.6 percent, the country's population will double roughly every 27 years. National and international agencies, which believe that high birth rates increase poverty and weaken social services, are encouraging Guatemalans to have fewer children. However, these agencies have been more successful in urban areas than in small, rural villages, where more than half of the people live.

Indians and Ladinos

Modern Guatemalans are considered to be either Indians or *ladinos*. These two primary social groups are based mainly on lifestyle rather than on ethnic background. If a person's lifestyle is most influenced by Spanish ways—that is, if the person speaks a non-Indian language and lives and dresses like most city dwellers—he or she is ladino. Most Guatemalans of Spanish descent are ladinos, as are many native people. Otherwise, if a person follows a traditional Mayan or other native lifestyle, he or she is considered Indian.

About half of all Guatemalans are direct descendants of the native people. Most Guatemalan Indians are Mayan, but other groups, such as the Xinca Indians, also live in Guatemala. The Maya themselves consist of the main group as well as subgroups such as the Quiché and Cakchiquel.

The lives of many native Guatemalans are much like those of their ancestors. For instance, most Indians speak at least one of the ancient

Mayan languages. Like the ancient Maya, most are farmers, although many modern Maya live in small, rural villages established during the colonial period. Located primarily in the western highlands, these villages are all similar in structure. At the center is a church, which faces a shady square. A well where people can get fresh water is usually located near the square, and shops and government buildings are located along the sides of the square. Some villagers build traditional houses from cornstalks that have been bound tightly together and topped with a thatched roof. Other Maya build homes of adobe (sun-dried clay bricks), stone, or concrete blocks, if they can afford them. These houses may have tile, thatched, or corrugated-tin roofs. In the lowlands, the houses are sometimes raised up from the ground to protect the foundations from moisture. In urban areas, the very poor live in huts or lean-tos made of wood, metal, or cardboard.

Most Mayan villages have no running water, and although electricity is available in most areas, many Indians cannot afford it. Women and children gather firewood for fuel and carry water from wells or rivers and streams. Mayan women have traditionally stayed in the home, doing the cooking, cleaning, weaving, and caring for the children. During the day, they may also walk to where their husbands are working to bring them meals.

A worker uses concrete blocks to enlarge a building in Ciudad Vieja.

Vegetables are plentiful on **market day in Antigua.**

In addition to farming, weekly and monthly village market days have become important to modern Indians. Some families grow more food than they can eat and sell the extra at the market. A growing tourist trade is also a source of income. Many Maya are excellent craftspeople and are able to sell their work at markets. In fact, the ability to earn extra money by selling their needlework and other finely crafted items to tourists has given Mayan women higher status and more independence in the household. Their income may make it unnecessary for their children to work to help support the families, freeing them to attend school.

Nearly all Spanish-heritage Guatemalans are ladinos. However, some native people become ladinos by leaving their villages and adopting less traditional lifestyles. Some of these people have chosen to follow a ladino lifestyle, while others have been forced into it by poverty and the need for jobs. To get work, the Maya are often pressured to give up their traditional clothing and to speak Spanish. Ladinos from Indian families may be seen as traitors to their culture and rejected by their families. In additon, most mestizos lead ladino lifestyles.

Most ladinos live in Guatemala City or in cities on the Pacific coastal plain or in the Caribbean coastal lowlands. Some are farmers or day laborers. Many live in small adobe houses, with roofs made from basic materials such as palm leaves. Some of them face challenges similar to those of people living in their villages, with reduced opportunities and influence in the government. Other ladinos make up the middle and upper-middle economic classes, working in business, industry, and government. These ladinos generally have more access to running water, electricity, hospitals, higher education, and other services than people in rural areas. Some of these ladinos can afford television sets, cars, and other goods. A few of them, especially those with family ties to the Spanish colonialists and the military, are very wealthy and play top roles in Guatemala's government and economy.

Among Guatemala's ethnic minorities are the Garífuna, descendants of the Carib Indians of the Caribbean Islands and African slaves. Almost 20,000 Garífuna, also called Black Caribs, live in Guatemala, most of them in Puerto Barrios on the Caribbean coast. About another 2 percent of Guatemala's population comes from other countries, such as Great Britain, Germany, and the United States.

Standard of Living

Modern Guatemala is estimated to have the lowest standard of living in Central America, and some studies conclude that it is among the worst in the Western Hemisphere. At least 60 percent of the population lives in extreme poverty, surviving on less than $2 per day. Most of these people live in rural areas and shantytowns (rundown areas usually filled with makeshift housing) in or around Guatemala City. It is believed that another 20 to 30 percent of Guatemalans live just above the level of extreme poverty. The minimum wage for agricultural workers is below $3 per day and slightly above $3 for other workers. The average annual income of all workers is estimated at $1,690. In addition, the official unemployment estimate is 7.5 percent. However, many more Guatemalans are underemployed, meaning they do not get enough work to support themselves adequately.

MAKING ENDS MEET

Some economists describe people who often do not have enough money to buy a basic basket of food as living in extreme poverty. People who cannot buy a basket of both goods and services are living below the poverty line.

Many of Guatemala's people fall into these categories, especially since local prices can be high compared to wages. For example, a bus ticket for the five-hour trip from Guatemala City to Puerto Barrios costs $6—or two days labor for an average Guatemalan worker. One night's stay in a *hospedaje* (often a room in a family's home) costs about $2 or $3.

Nutrition and Health Care

Poor nutrition and health care contribute to Guatemala's low standard of living. Many poor Guatemalans, especially in rural areas, grow some or all of their own food. However, their diets are often lacking essential elements, and malnutrition among the poor is very common. One of the results of inadequate diet is a high rate of infant mortality. Pregnant women who are malnourished often have babies that have low birth weights and are therefore more vulnerable to illnesses. In Guatemala 41 out of every 1,000 babies die before the age of one, compared to 10 out of 1,000 in Costa Rica. In addition, Guatemala's life expectancy is among the lowest in Central America, with women's life expectancy at 69 years and men's at 63. However, these figures are averages, and the life expectancy of Guatemalan Indians is estimated to be 10 to 15 years lower than that of ladinos.

This difference between ladinos' and Indians' life expectancy is partly because the rural Indian population has little access to modern health care. A few clinics are located in the countryside, but they are generally underfunded and understaffed and have little impact on the people's health. Most formally trained doctors practice in Guatemala City at public hospitals, and people with enough money go to private clinics. But most Indians either treat themselves using traditional folk medicines or consult villagers with medical knowledge.

Some Indians go to *curanderas*, Catholic female **healers** who treat both the spirits and the bodies of their patients. Some curanderas, called *parteras*, specialize in helping women during childbirth. Other Indians consult male healers called shamans. Like the curanderas, shamans try to heal patients both spiritually and physically. They also play a religious role and are believed to be able to communicate with ancestors and with Mayan gods and goddesses.

A lack of clean water is a major health problem in Guatemala. Only about 70 to 80 percent of the general population has access to safe drinking water, and the percentage slips to about 50 percent in rural areas. This situation places people at risk for waterborne parasites and diseases such as cholera. Poor sanitation and industrial and agricultural pollution are also damaging to public health. And because most people do not get the shots that they need, many poor children in both rural and urban areas suffer from preventable diseases such as measles and whooping cough.

Insect-borne tropical diseases such as malaria, dengue, and yellow fever pose a major health risk to Guatemalans as well. Because antibiotics, vaccines, and other medications are not available to many

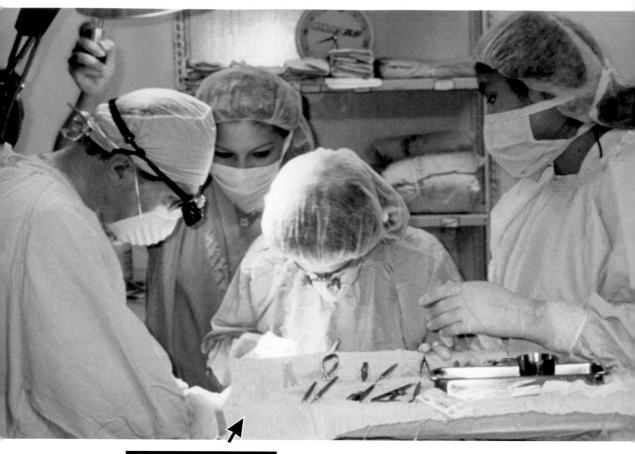

The **Rodolfo Robles hospitals** in Guatemala City and Quetzaltenango may specialize in treating visual and hearing impairments. Staff members also teach nutrition, first aid, family planning, and the prevention of sexually transmitted diseases.

people, these and other curable conditions, such as hepatitis and pneumonia, often go untreated. A lack of information also puts the population at risk of contracting the human immunodeficiency virus (HIV), the virus that can cause acquired immunodeficiency syndrome (AIDS). To prevent an epidemic, international and local organizations are trying to educate the Guatemalan population about how HIV is passed from person to person through bodily fluids, but as of 2003, more than 73,000 cases of the disease had already been reported in Guatemala.

Another problem threatening Guatemalans' health is drug abuse. The country is a passageway for illegal drugs, such as cocaine, heroin, and opium, that are being smuggled to North America. As a result, drug use, especially of cocaine, is rising among local residents. National and international law enforcement groups are working to crack down on the drug trade through Guatemala.

Education

Guatemala's first university was established in 1676 by Catholic priests. The Catholic Church also established schools for children. Most of these schools were for Spanish families only, but some were set aside for the native population. After Guatemala won its independence, one of the new government's goals was to provide schools for all children. But cost, cultural differences, and a lack of bilingual teachers made this goal difficult to achieve, and adequate education is still inaccessible to many Guatemalans.

Modern Guatemala officially provides free public education for all children aged 7 to 14. However, fewer than half of Guatemalan children attend elementary school, and most of those do not finish. According to a 2000 report by the United Nations, Guatemalan children attend school for an average of only 2.3 years. In rural areas, the number drops to 1.3 years. As a result, the national literacy rate is estimated to be between 55 percent and 69 percent—among the lowest in Central America.

Indian children sometimes face special obstacles in getting an education. Rural families have traditionally resisted sending their children to school because they are needed at home to help with the farming. In addition, while most classes are taught in Spanish, many Mayan children know only their native languages. Due to this language barrier, the rate of illiteracy among Indians is higher than the national percentage. It is even higher among females, who are sometimes not encouraged to go to school. Things are changing for the better, however. In 1988 the government formally recognized the Academy of Mayan Languages, an organization that works to preserve Guatemala's native languages. Indian children became able to attend lessons taught in their own language. Literacy rates are beginning to rise, and more Indians have enrolled at colleges and universities.

Many Mayan languages were traditionally oral only, with no written form. To help Mayan children learn their lessons, scholars, teachers, and members of the **Academy of Mayan Languages** began to develop writing systems for these languages. This work made it possible to publish textbooks and other tools in students' native languages.

CULTURAL LIFE

Guatemala's blend of native traditions with Spanish customs has given this nation a unique and vibrant cultural life. From colorful Mayan markets, music, and stories to stately colonial buildings, the Spanish language, and Catholic holidays, Guatemala offers a rich array of cultural treasure.

▶ Clothing and Food

Although ladinos wear modern European-style dress, such as blue jeans and business suits, many Maya still wear the traditional dress known as *traje.* Every native village's traje has its own unique colors and designs. These garments are woven in brilliant colors and complex patterns. The designs embroidered on them are often taken from Mayan myth and symbols, but sometimes they are of modern objects such as rockets.

The *huipil,* a long, loose-fitting blouse, is the most important part of a woman's clothing. No two huipils are the same, and they take many hours to make. Beneath the huipil is a long skirt. A woman's headdress,

made of colorful strips of cloth and wrapped around the head, is also an important part of the customary dress. Some women wear brimmed hats, usually made of wool.

Traditional dress for men consists of short, loose pants, which are sometimes brightly striped, and an intricately embroidered cotton shirt. A Mayan man may also wear a small woolen blanket, called a *rodillera*, wrapped around his waist. Sometimes a poncholike garment is worn over the shoulders and held in place by a colorful sash tied at the waist. Many men also wear straw hats with wide brims. Men's sandals are usually similar in design to those worn by the ancient Maya. Some Mayan men who wear modern clothing still wear brightly colored sashes around their waists to honor their culture.

Like many parts of Guatemalan culture, the nation's cuisine is a mixture of traditional and Spanish tastes. Black beans have been a big part of diets for hundreds of years, while rice was introduced by Spanish settlers and quickly became a staple. Another typical food is the tortilla, a flat,

PLÁTANOS AL HORNO (BAKED PLANTAINS)

These sweet treats are typically Guatemalan.

2 tablespoons sugar

1 teaspoon ground cinnamon

2 ripe plantains, with black skins

2 tablespoons butter

cream and honey for topping

1. Preheat oven to 350°F (175°C).
2. In a small bowl, combine sugar and cinnamon.
3. Use a sharp knife to trim off each end of plantains. Slit the peel lengthwise, from one end of the plantain to the other, on opposite sides. Use your fingers to remove peel. Then split each plantain open lengthwise, but try not to cut completely in half.
4. Sprinkle plantains inside and out with the sugar mixture and dab some butter into the slits. Coat a baking dish with butter and place plantains in dish. Bake 20 to 30 minutes, or until soft and brown. Serve warm with fresh cream and honey.

Serves 2 to 4.

thin pancake made from cornmeal. Tortillas accompany most meals and are sometimes stuffed with vegetables or, if it is affordable, spiced meat. *Pepian* is a popular stew of chicken, peppers, potatoes, and pumpkin seeds. For dessert, Guatemalan diners might enjoy baked or fried plantains (similar to bananas) served with honey and cream. Overall, a greater variety of foods is available in cities than in rural areas. Meats are eaten regularly by the wealthy but may be too expensive for the poor, who eat mostly beans, rice, and eggs.

Religion

When Catholics arrived in Guatemala, the Maya had an ancient religion honoring more than 160 deities (gods and goddesses). Mayan deities represented all elements of the natural world, such as the sun, moon, rivers, and mountains. The Maya also worshiped gods symbolizing elements of their daily routines, including work such as weaving and necessities such as medicine and corn. Every day had some religious significance, and many days throughout the

year were set aside to honor partic-
ular gods and goddesses through
ceremonies and tributes.

The Spanish colonial government and the Catholic Church
both hoped to convert the Maya
to Christianity. They destroyed
many Mayan temples, sculptures,
and sacred texts, and forced
native Guatemalans to practice
Catholicism. Some Indians con-
verted willingly to Christianity,
while others quietly kept alive the
beliefs and traditions of their
ancestors. The result was a unique
blend of traditional Mayan beliefs
and Christian ideas.

This blending was made easier
by the fact that Christianity and
the Mayan religion already had
some striking similarities. A

Modern Mayan priests sit beside a
decorated statue at a ceremony in
Santiago Atitlán.

RELIGIOUS RITES

To please their gods, Mayan
worshipers sometimes
sacrificed the life of an
animal, such as a deer.
Sometimes they also
sacrificed humans—usually
in times of distress, such as
earthquakes or famines. The
Maya also gave their own
blood as a tribute to the
gods, puncturing their
tongues or other parts of
their bodies. Cannibalism
(eating human flesh) was
part of some ceremonies.

The Maya also had
important burial rites. They
sometimes painted the body
of the deceased red and
placed it with a few
valued objects for use
in the next world. The
body and the objects
were rolled up in a
straw mat and buried
beneath the dirt floor
of the house. People
of great stature, such
as the chiefs, were
buried within the
Mayan pyramids, along
with valuables and
items useful in their
daily lives. Sometimes,
their servants were
sacrificed and buried
with them.

Mayan symbol indicating the four directions on the earth, for instance, is very similar to the Christian cross. In addition, the saints that Catholics honor soon merged with many Mayan gods and goddesses. While these unique Guatemalan saints have Christian names, local statues and paintings of them often resemble Mayan deities. The Maya also believed in an eternal spirit, similar to the Catholic idea of the soul, and that after death a person passed from the earth to a heaven or hell.

Many modern Indians still practice this blend of religions, while most ladinos practice more traditional Catholicism. Roman Catholicism is by far the most common religion in Guatemala, but other branches of Christianity have also sent missionaries to work with the poor. Small communities of Jews and Muslims also live in Guatemala.

Holidays and Festivals

Many religious festivals, or *fiestas*, take place during the Guatemalan year. A whole series of celebrations in anticipation of Christmas begins at the end of October. These fiestas include processions, traditional dances, and favorite foods, such as tamales (stuffed cornmeal packets), sweet breads, and chocolate. Christmastime celebrations continue until February, when people take down their *nacimientos* (household displays representing the scene of Jesus' birth) and store them away for the next year.

A holiday procession to a shrine *(far left)* in Antigua draws a crowd.

Specific activities differ throughout the country, but Guatemalans love fireworks, and they are a part of any fiesta, even among the very poor. Kite flying is also popular, especially for All Souls' Day (also known as Day of the Dead), celebrated on November 2. Many believe that the kites flown in local cemeteries carry messages to the dead and help guide their souls to heaven.

Guatemala's most important celebrations are held during Holy Week, or Semana Santa, the seven days before Easter Sunday. Throughout the country, people carry statues of Jesus and the saints in elaborate processions from their local churches and through the streets. Huge floats are made in honor of the saints, and events from Jesus' life are reenacted through dance and short plays. In preparation for the processions, people use brightly colored flower petals, leaves, fruit, and dyed sand or sawdust to create designs in the streets or sidewalks in front of their homes. Called *alfombras,* the Spanish word for carpets, these designs incorporate Christian, Mayan, and other patterns.

Many secular (non-religious) holidays are also celebrated in Guatemala. These include Labor Day on May 1, Independence Day on September 15, and New Year's Day on January 1.

Two Guatemalan youths **construct alfombras** for Semana Santa. Others decorate a nearby building.

◉ Arts and Crafts

The Maya of the Classic Period were master architects. They built cities of huge pyramids, temples, and palaces. They placed massive stone structures so precisely that they could be used to measure the movement of the sun, moon, and planets. Glyphs carved into the sides of stele (stone columns or slabs) recorded important events, as did realistic human portraits cut into temple walls. Mayan artists painted palace walls with colorful murals depicting battle scenes and ceremonies, and created small carved sculptures and beautifully decorated pottery.

Modern Maya express their creativity through many arts and crafts, such as silver work and pottery making. However, the most important Mayan craft is weaving. Women often weave cloth on small, portable looms called backstraps, while men usually use bigger looms, operated by foot, to produce larger quantities of material. The woven cloth is both beautiful and functional, and its traditional designs and colors help to preserve the heritage of the Indians. The blankets, rugs, clothing, and wall hangings that Mayan families sell on market days also bring villagers much-needed income.

The best weavers, such as this woman in San Antonio Aguas Calientes, can earn some money **demonstrating traditional weaving** on a backstrap loom for tourists.

Guatemala is also home to many fine artists, some of whose work shows the influence of both European and regional counterparts. Andrés Curruchich, for example, was born in 1891 and used the bright colors and mythology of his Mayan roots to develop a style of painting that was uniquely Guatemalan. Around the same time, Carmen Pettersen created watercolors that were similar in style to European works but depicted native people of her Guatemalan homeland. Elmar Rojas, born in 1940, studied painting in both Guatemala and Europe and has been honored as one of the world's best contemporary artists.

◉ Music and Dance

Music is another important form of cultural expression in Guatemala. The ancient Maya played drums, panpipes, ceramic whistles, and a mournful-sounding flute called a *chirima*. Another instrument closely associated with Guatemala is the marimba, a xylophone-like instrument that was brought to the Caribbean region from Africa. Marimbas, which may require four or five musicians to cover their wide range of notes, provide the music for most Guatemalan festivals. They may be accompanied by percussion instruments such as drums or rattles called *sonajas*.

Marimba players entertain hotel guests in Antigua.

Guatemalan youths fill a nightclub in Antigua to show off their skill in salsa, a Latin American dance performed to music that blends rock, jazz, and other sounds. For links where you can find out more about Guatemalan music, dance, holidays and festivals, crafts, cuisine, and much more, go to vgsbooks.com.

In addition to traditional music, classical European music is popular in Guatemala, and the National Symphony Orchestra is considered to be one of the best orchestras in Latin America. Reggae and rock, especially Punta Rock, also have many fans. Punta Rock originally began among the Garífuna of Belize and later spread to other Garífuna communities along the Caribbean coast. Its primary instrument is a hollow turtle shell played like a drum, but it also features other instruments such as the electric guitar.

Local festivals almost always feature dance performances reflecting the culture—or mix of cultures—of the village or city. One of these, El Baile de los Moros y Cristianos (Dance of the Moors and Christians), was performed in Spain in the twelfth century. Since then, native Guatemalans have added their own elements to the dance. The all-male cast wears elaborate costumes and masks, yelling out their lines as they dance and wage mock battles. This performance is an exercise in endurance, lasting for hours.

Literature and Film

Guatemala has a rich literary tradition. Despite the loss of most ancient Mayan books, a strong oral tradition and the protection and translation of a few Mayan texts have preserved some histories and myths. One of the most important works is the *Popol Vuh,* an epic of Mayan myth, symbolism, beliefs, and practices that influences many modern Guatemalan writers.

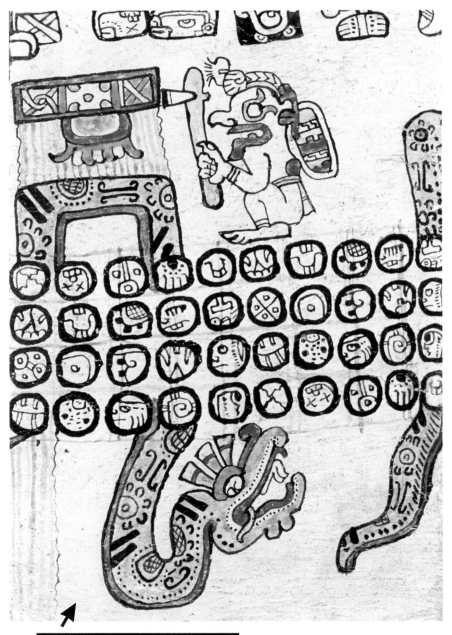

This **page from a Mayan codex, or book,** shows Quetzalcoatl (the Mayan god of agriculture and knowledge) as a feathered serpent.

The eighteenth-century poet Rafael Landívar wrote the epic poem *Rusticatio Mexicana*, describing the customs of rural Guatemalans. Landívar was a native of Antigua. However, he was forced to flee Guatemala when the Spanish tried to curb the growing power of the Jesuit order of Catholic priests to which he belonged.

As a result of the civil war's violent political struggles, modern Guatemalan literature is often highly charged with politics. Some authors are critical of both Guatemala's government and of foreign governments, such as the United States, that have sometimes had a negative influence on events in Guatemala. Such political novels include the 1946 book *El Señor Presidente (The President)*, by Nobel Prize winner Miguel Angel Asturias. Another is Francisco Goldman's *The Long Night of White Chickens* (1992), which depicts life in Guatemala under military control during the 1980s. Arturo Arias's novel *After the Bombs* (1979) is set in the early 1950s, at the peak of the United Fruit Company's power. His screenplay *El Norte (The North)*, which was made into a film in 1984, is a vivid account of Mayan life under military rule.

Other films made in Guatemala or by Guatemalan filmmakers include *Terremoto en Guatemala (Earthquake in Guatemala)*, about the destruction caused by the 1976 earthquake. During the civil war, many Guatemalan films were actually made in other countries or with the help of outside filmmakers, especially from Mexico. The 2001 film *La Palabra Desenterrada (Haunted Land)* tells the story of an Indian and a ladino who survived the civil war. *El Silencio de Neto (The Silence of Neto)*, made by the prominent Guatemalan director Luis Argueta, tells the story of a young boy living at the time of the 1954 coup and the turmoil that followed. Argueta's *Llamada por Cobrar (Collect Call)* depicts the challenges facing a boy who moves from rural Guatemala to New York City.

Sports and Entertainment

The kinds of entertainment that Guatemalans enjoy depend largely on their location and income. However, sports have been popular in Guatemala for centuries. The ancient Maya are believed by historians to have played a game called *pok-a-tok*. Playing on courts built specifically for the sport, two teams attempted to put a ball through a ring on a wall, similar to a modern basketball hoop. Pok-a-tok presented an extra challenge, however, as the players were not allowed to touch the ball with their hands or feet. Some scholars also think that losing players may have been put to death after the game.

In modern Guatemala, soccer is by far the most popular sport. Guatemala's National League has four teams in Guatemala City and

Guatemalan soccer player Martin Machon *(left, in blue and white)* leads Guatemala to a victory over Costa Rica in a 2000 World Cup qualifying match in Mazatenango.

others across the country, and one of the sport's greatest local stars is Carlos Ruiz Gutierrez. Basketball and baseball also draw some fans.

In most Maya villages, a major source of entertainment is the many festivals held throughout the year, which involve the entire community. Fishing in the nation's oceans or lakes and streams is also popular, although for many Guatemalans it is a way to provide food for their families rather than a sport.

THE ECONOMY

Despite many changes in leadership and the human and economic costs of the civil war, Guatemala's economy is growing. The 1996 peace accords, especially, helped to stabilize business and industry and renew the confidence of foreign investors.

The most important part of the economy continues to be agricultural exports, which account for about 25 percent of Guatemala's gross domestic product (GDP) of $48.3 billion. Approximately two-thirds of Guatemala's exports are agricultural, and about half of the country's labor force works on plantations, farms, and ranches. In addition to the main export crops of coffee, sugar, and bananas, other important export crops are cotton, corn, cattle, the spice cardamom, flowers, vegetables, and rice. Nonagricultural exports include timber, rubber, and crude oil. More than half of Guatemala's exports go to the United States. El Salvador, Honduras, Costa Rica, and Germany are other important trading partners.

The services sector employs around 35 percent of Guatemala's workforce and includes jobs such as tour guides, restaurant workers, and bank

tellers. Industry makes up most of the remaining workforce. Jobs in this sector include sugar refining and the manufacture of textiles, clothing, furniture, chemicals, petroleum, metals, rubber, and medical products.

Agriculture

Throughout the late 1800s and much of the 1900s, Guatemalan agriculture was largely devoted to bananas. The United Fruit Company acquired large amounts of coastal land, where bananas grow well. The United Fruit Company was good for Guatemala in some ways. Its crops stimulated the economy, and its plantations provided jobs and schools. The company also funded research into preventing tropical diseases. But United Fruit grew so powerful that it virtually controlled the entire Guatemalan economy. By the early 1950s, when United Fruit helped spur Jacobo Arbenz Guzmán's overthrow, the company proved to have significant political influence, as well. Although United Fruit's power eventually lessened, the

A coffee plantation in the highlands near Antigua

company still exists in Central America, under the name Chiquita Brands International.

In present-day Guatemala, coffee is the nation's most important crop. It is grown mainly in the western and central highlands, on plantations established by German immigrants in the 1800s. The practice of warming the trees by burning fires in the orchards gives the coffee a distinctive smoky taste. When the international economy is strong, Guatemala's high-quality arabica beans are in great demand, and coffee has enriched some Guatemalans and has benefited the overall economy.

However, the coffee industry has also had negative effects. Many Indians were forced off of fertile lands to make room for plantations. The industry's expansion has contributed to deforestation and soil erosion, and some of the country's four thousand coffee-processing plants have polluted streams and lakes. Plantation owners, who have great influence on government policies, may discourage land reform and environmental restrictions. In addition, heavy reliance on one crop is risky. Any prolonged decline in world coffee prices would hurt Guatemala's entire economy.

On a much smaller scale than the vast coffee plantations, family farming employs and feeds most Guatemalans. Although some farmers grow only enough to feed their families, others are able to grow enough extra to sell or trade at market. Many other agricultural industries are becoming more important as well. For example, the production and export of fruits, particularly berries, has increased dramatically. Berries, together with other fruits and preserves, brought in $3.5 million from foreign markets. Cut flowers, another growing market, brought in $32.8 million.

Fishing and Forestry

With two coastlines, fishing is a natural part of Guatemala's economy. In the early 2000s, the nation began trying to increase its fishing industry along the Pacific Coast. Fish-processing plants export more than $10 million worth of shrimp, fish, and lobsters, and sales are predicted to rise further.

Wood, including valuable mahogany, is another of the country's important exports. However, while the forestry industry benefits the national and local economies, it often contributes to deforestation and soil

Mahogany trees have been harvested since the 1500s for their rich, red-brown wood, prized in making furniture.

erosion. Striking the delicate balance between meeting economic needs and protecting the environment is one of Guatemala's ongoing challenges.

> Many Guatemalan products can be extracted from trees without harming them—balsam, medicinal oils and barks, cinnamon, allspice, vanilla, sarsaparilla, camphor, and chicle (used in chewing gum), for example. Guatemala's chicle is ranked the best in the world. To find the latest information on the Guatemalan economy, go to vgsbooks.com.

Mining and Manufacturing

Guatemala has substantial deposits of nickel, copper, and other minerals. However, because they are often hard to reach and mine, they have not played a large role in the country's economy. Oil reserves in northern Petén, on the other hand, have great potential. Since the end of the civil war, the Guatemalan government has begun to allow large oil companies to explore the region, and geologists believe that significant reserves of both oil and natural gas may be found. Although conservationists are concerned about the environmental effects of further drilling, oil production would enable Guatemala to export oil rather than importing it as it has historically done.

Manufacturing also contributes to Guatemala's economy. In the textile industry, foreign-owned garment businesses have grown rapidly in number. Pieces of garments are imported and assembled locally in plants, shops, and homes. The finished clothes are then exported. Although this industry provides badly needed jobs, many workplaces are uncomfortable or even unsafe. These substandard factories are called *maquiladoras,* a Spanish term for sweatshops.

SWEATSHOPS

Designer clothing makers from around the world have been criticized for unethical labor practices in Guatemala and other poor countries. They've been accused of overworking their employees, allowing hazardous conditions in the workplace, hiring children, and paying very low wages. International human-rights agencies are working to close down such sweatshops—by making the public aware of such practices.

At a factory in Antigua, **factory workers polish jadeite,** the type of jade mined in Guatemala. Jadeite can only be cut with a diamond or stainless steel blade. Many craftspeople create both beautiful modern jewelry and replicas of ancient jade objects to sell.

Transportation and Communication

Although rural Guatemala still lacks many modern conveniences, the country has worked to improve its transportation system. More than 2,000 miles (3,219 km) of paved roads stretch across the country, including two major highways—the Pacific Highway along the western coast and the Pan-American Highway through Guatemala City and the highlands. A national railway also carries people from place to place, and international airports are located in Guatemala City and Flores.

Guatemalans get information from more than half a dozen newspapers, as well as from five television stations and more than eighty-five radio stations. Some of these information sources are privately owned, while others are run by the government. Although Guatemala's constitution technically protects freedom of speech and freedom of the press, the government has been accused of controlling and censoring information put out by private sources.

A colorful tour bus waits to fill with **tourists in Guatemala City.**

Tourism and Additional Money Sources

Tourism, the fastest growing part of Guatemala's economy, has great potential to both preserve the nation's archaeological, environmental, and scenic treasures and to bring it profit. Other Central American countries such as Belize have successfully promoted ecotourism, which allows people to visit protected areas and local villages without disturbing or damaging them. In addition to creating a market for lodging, food, transportation, and guides, many tourists buy arts and crafts directly from the Indians at marketplaces, providing local economies with a boost.

Guatemala's economy is also aided by outside funds. A major source of income is the money sent home by Guatemalans working outside the country, especially in the United States and Canada. This money is estimated to total more than $500 million annually. In addition, Guatemala receives economic help from countries including the United States, Japan, France, Italy, and Germany. International financial agencies, such as the Inter-American Development Bank, also provide loans. These loans help Guatemala in the short term, but they also build up a huge foreign debt. Guatemala's foreign debt stands at about $4.5 billion and continues to grow. As lenders press the government to pay back its loans, Guatemala will have less money to spend on domestic needs.

The Future

In many ways, Guatemala is still a country in crisis. Many observers claim that the government represents only a small number of its people and that the right-wing military is still in control. Guatemala's future will be determined largely by its ability to make reforms, especially in the distribution of land and power, to better serve all of its citizens.

The 1996 peace accords were a huge step toward the nation's rebuilding. In addition to ending the thirty-six-year civil war, the accords required the government to provide health care, education, and other basic services for the rural population. They also guaranteed the right of the native people to participate in deciding local and national policies. Since then, the election process in Guatemala has improved. Although overall voter turnout at elections in 1999 was low, the number of women and Indian voters was the highest in recent history. Nevertheless, access to certain rural voting places is still considered inadequate.

The Guatemalan government has also worked to make the nation competitive in the world economy. Guatemala attracts investments from foreign countries, such as Mexico and Spain, to develop domestic services such as transportation and communication. Other economic issues that need attention are the rising cost of consumer goods and the growing national debt.

Yet to achieve any real economic or social security, the government must keep peace among its people and protect them from violence. This goal includes bringing human-rights offenders to justice and preventing future abuses. Many human-rights activists, judges, lawyers, reporters, and other Guatemalans still feel at risk from the military and other forces in the country. Meanwhile, investigators continue to study findings taken from mass graves of the civil war's victims. Guatemala's human rights record is improving, however, due to efforts of its own citizens and of international agencies that monitor abuse. Foreign aid from the United States and other governments, for example, often depends upon Guatemala's acceptance of basic standards of human rights.

The government must also take action against street crime. Guns left over from the war are easy to come by, and carjacking has become so common that drivers of delivery trucks often hire armed guards. Guatemala has also become a channel for smuggling heroin, cocaine, and other illegal drugs from South and Central America to the United States.

Many Guatemalans were dismayed when Efrain Ríos Montt declared his candidacy for president in the 2003 election because they feared a return to a government controlled by the military. But voters rejected Montt and elected Oscar Berger, the conservative former mayor of Guatemala City. In his first news conference, Berger promised a government that would bring justice—as well as education, clean water, and health care—to every village in Guatemala. While Guatemalans hope for such improvements, they worry that Berger will fail to fulfill all of his pledges.

Despite Guatemala's many challenges, it also has a great many resources upon which to draw. Its people are strong and diverse, and its land is rich in natural and historical treasures. If it can achieve its potential to become a peaceful, democratic society, it may indeed grow into a Land of Eternal Spring.

1000s B.C.	Indigenous Guatemalans set up early farming in the highlands.
A.D. 250-900	Classic Period of Mayan civilization
1523-1524	The Spanish conquistador Pedro de Alvarado defeats the Maya. Spanish colonialism begins in Guatemala and throughout Central America and Mexico.
1543	Antigua is established as Spain's colonial capital after an earthquake destroys the first capital, Santiago de los Caballeros.
1676	The University of San Carlos, Guatemala's first university, opens.
1720	The Spanish monarchy declares an end to the practice of encomienda, which forced the native population to work for the colonists without compensation.
1776	The colonial capital is moved to Guatemala City after an earthquake destroys Antigua.
1821	Guatemala declares its independence from Spain.
1839	Guatemala officially declares itself an independent nation. The conservative president Rafael Carrera takes power.
1871	Civil uprisings bring Miguel García Granados to office.
1898	Manuel Estrada Cabrera takes power.
1901	Estrada grants the United Fruit Company the exclusive right to transport postal mail between Guatemala and the United States, and the United Fruit Company begins exporting tropical fruit from Guatemala.
1931	Jorge Ubico Castañeda saves Guatemala's economy partly by granting foreign businesses many privileges.
1944	Liberal Juan José Arévalo Bermejo is elected, bringing a decade of reform known as the Ten Years of Spring.
1954	A U.S.-backed coup replaces Jacobo Arbenz Guzmán with the military dictator Carlos Castillo Armas. Liberal reforms are overturned.
1961	A civil war begins between Guatemalan military forces and revolutionaries.
1967	Miguel Angel Asturias wins the Nobel Prize for Literature.
1976	A major earthquake strikes, killing thousands of Guatemalans and destroying the homes of many others.

1982   A military coup returns Guatemala to military dictatorship under General José Efraín Rios Montt. Rios Montt oversees the worst period of human-rights abuse in the country's recent history, as the civil war continues.

1985   The first civilian president in fifteen years is elected.

1989   Mexico and Guatemala agree to make Petén's rain forests part of the Maya Biosphere Reserve.

1991   Negotiations to end the civil war take place between the Guatemalan government and the Guatemalan National Revolutionary Union.

1992   Rigoberta Menchú Tum, a Mayan woman, is awarded the Nobel Peace Prize following publication of her memoirs of the war.

1994   The Guatemalan government and rebel groups agree to peace accords mandating reforms. Conservatives win the elections. Luis Argueta's *The Silence of Neto* becomes the first Guatemalan film to be distributed internationally.

1996   A cease-fire officially ends the civil war.

1998   Human-rights activist Bishop Juan Gerardi Conedera is murdered.

1999   The United Nations estimates that 200,000 Guatemalans died during the civil war. The UN report concludes that 93 percent of human-rights violations were committed by the military government and that the government oversaw the massacre of more than 600 Mayan villagers.

2000   Alfonso Portillo Cabrera steps into office as president. Guatemalan Evelyn López wins the Queen of the Year international beauty pageant. One of her outfits was the traditional Mayan traje.

2002   Carlos Ruiz Gutierrez leads the Guatemalan soccer team to the second round of World Cup preliminaries.

2003   Oscar Berger, the conservative former mayor of Guatemala City, defeats Rios Montt in his run for the presidency. Berger invites human rights' activist Rigoberta Menchú to join his government in working toward justice for all Guatemalans. The Guatemalan government recognizes Chalchiteco, the twenty-second officially acknowledged Mayan language.

COUNTRY NAME Republic of Guatemala

AREA 42,042 square miles (108,889 sq. km)

MAIN LANDFORMS Sierra Madre, Altos Cuchumatanes Mountains, Volcán Tajumulco, Petén, Caribbean coastal lowlands, Pacific coastal plain

HIGHEST POINT Volcán Tajumulco, 13,845 feet (4,220 m) above sea level

LOWEST POINT Sea level

MAJOR RIVERS Motagua, Dulce, Sarstoon, Suchiate

ANIMALS Deer, wild pigs, tapirs, armadillos, ocelots, bears, alligators, monkeys, quetzals, toucans, fer-de-lance, boa constrictors

CAPITAL CITY Guatemala City

OTHER MAJOR CITIES Antigua, Chichicastenango, Escuintla, Flores, Puerto Barrios, Quetzaltenango

OFFICIAL LANGUAGE Spanish

MONETARY UNIT Quetzal. 1 quetzal = 100 centavos.

GUATEMALAN CURRENCY

Guatemala's unit of currency is named after the country's rare national bird, the quetzal. "Quetzal" is abbreviated as QTD, or simply Q. Individual banknotes are available in values of Q100, Q50, Q20, Q10, Q5, and Q1.

Coins are in units of centavos. One hundred centavos make up a quetzal, and coins come in values of 1, 5, and 25 centavos. Only a few coins with values of less than 25 centavos are still in circulation. In 1996 a special Q1 coin was introduced to commemorate the peace accords.

Fast Facts

Currency

The Guatemalan flag has three broad, vertical stripes. The light blue stripes on the left and right represent the Caribbean Sea and the Pacific Ocean. The Guatemalan coat of arms on the white middle stripe displays the quetzal bird, representing freedom. The coat of arms also shows crossed rifles and swords, circled by a wreath. Resting on the wreath is a scroll with the following inscription: Libertad 15 de Septiembre de 1821. This is the date, in Spanish, of Guatemala's independence from Spain.

Guatemala's national anthem is "Guatemala Feliz," called "Fortunate Guatemala" or "Guatemala Be Praised" in English. The song was the winning entry in a contest held by the government in 1896. The words were written by José Joaquín Palma, and the music was written by Rafael Alvárez Ovalle.

Guatemala Feliz
Fortunate Guatemala! May your altars
Never be profaned by cruel men.
May there never be slaves who submit to their yoke,
Or tyrants who deride you.
If tomorrow your sacred soil
Should be threatened by foreign invasion,
Your fair flag, flying freely in the wind,
Will call to you: Conquer or die.

Your fair flag, flying freely in the wind,
Will call to you: Conquer or die.
For your people, with heart and soul,
Would prefer death to slavery.

For a link where you can listen to Guatemala's national anthem, "Guatemala Feliz," go to vgsbooks.com.

Flag

National Anthem

PEDRO DE ALVARADO (ca. 1485–1541) Born in Badajoz, Spain, Alvarado was a conquistador who came to the Americas with Hernán Cortés in 1519. After helping Cortés conquer the Aztecs in Mexico, Alvarado went on to conquer the Maya in 1523, beginning three hundred years of colonial rule in Guatemala. Alvarado and his family were the first Europeans to govern the country.

JUAN JOSÉ ARÉVALO BERMEJO (1904–1990) Born in Taxisco, Arévalo was elected Guatemala's president in 1944 and held office until 1950. His liberal administration began the period known as the Ten Years of Spring, during which many reforms were made to help the poor and the Maya. However, after Arévalo's successor was removed from office by a coup, Arévalo's reforms were overturned by the military dictators who seized control.

LUIS ARGUETA (b. 1946) Argueta is a film director and screenwriter who was born in Guatemala City. He traveled to the United States to study engineering and went on to study film. In 1978 he filmed his first documentary, the award-winning *The Cost of Cotton*. He also cowrote and directed *The Silence of Neto* (1994), which was recognized as the first Guatemalan film to be shown internationally.

MIGUEL ANGEL ASTURIAS (1899–1974) Winner of the Nobel Prize for Literature in 1967, Asturias was born in Guatemala City. He studied law in college and co-founded the Popular University of Guatemala, a school intended for poorer Guatemalans who could not otherwise afford to go to college. Asturias lived in Europe for much of his life, in part because Guatemala's more conservative leaders during his lifetime disliked his political writings, including the novel *El Señor Presidente (The President)*. Other works by Asturias include the poetry collection *Sien de Alondra (Temple of the Lark)* and the novel *Viento Fuerte (Strong Wind)*.

JUSTO RUFINO BARRIOS (1825–1885) Born in the village of San Lorenzo, Barrios first went to college to become a lawyer but later ended up as a military leader. After becoming president in 1872, Barrios made a number of reforms limiting the privileges of the church and the wealthy. The Catholic Church excommunicated Barrios (barred him from the church) for transferring large tracts of land from the church to foreign coffee growers.

RAFAEL CARRERA (1814–1865) Carrera was born in Guatemala City and had a mixed Spanish and Indian heritage. Barely able to read and write, he managed to gain power after Guatemala became independent. He was named president in 1851. Three years later, he appointed himself president for life and remained dictator until his death.

CALIXTA GABRIEL XIQUÍN (b. 1956) This Mayan poetess and teacher was born in a village near San José Poaquil. When the civil war began, she witnessed the destruction of her home and the military's kidnapping and murder of many Maya—including her three brothers. Under the pen name Caly Domitila Kanek, she began writing poetry in her native Mayan language. Her work, which describes her own family's suffering and the problems facing all Maya, was not published in Guatemala until after the 1996 peace accords. Xiquín continues to write and to work for peace and for the human rights of the Maya.

HASAW CHAN K'AWIL (ca. late A.D. 600s–734) Also known as Ah Cacau and Lord Chocolate, Hasaw Chan K'awil was the greatest ruler of the Mayan city-state Tikal. Taking the throne in 682, when the city was in a state of decline, Hasaw Chan K'awil began restoring Tikal. He oversaw the construction of many grand temples and pyramids near the Great Plaza, many of which can still be seen by modern tourists. He also conquered a rival Mayan state, expanding Tikal's military and political power. When he died, Hasaw Chan K'awil was buried in a magnificent tomb under a 145-foot-high (44-m) pyramid topped with a temple.

RIGOBERTA MENCHÚ TUM (b. 1959) Born in the village of Chimel, Menchú is a Mayan woman who wrote a memoir of the civil war from the perspective of an Indian. The work brought the world's attention to Guatemala's native people, and Menchú was awarded the Nobel Peace Prize in 1992. Although the truth of her account has been publicly questioned, raising major controversy, Menchú remains a powerful symbol of the Maya in Guatemala.

ALFONSO PORTILLO CABRERA (b. 1951) Born in Zacapa, Portillo was elected president in 1999. He immediately forced senior military officers who may have been responsible for wartime human-rights violations to retire. He also proposed laws to limit the military's power. However, Portillo's right-wing political party, the Guatemalan Republican Front, is still associated with known human-rights abusers.

JOSÉ EFRAÍN RÍOS MONTT (b. 1926) Known as "The General," Ríos Montt became a powerful military leader after attending the military academy School of the Americas in Panama. He seized control of the Guatemalan government in 1982, and under his administration, human-rights violations, especially against the Maya, hit their peak. Despite this record, Ríos Montt remains active in Guatemalan politics.

CARLOS RUIZ GUTIERREZ (b. 1979) Ruiz was born in Guatemala City and began playing soccer when he was twelve. He was captain of the 2000 Guatemalan Olympic team, and he made eight goals for the Guatemalan National Team to qualify for the second round of the 2002 World Cup. In 2002 Ruiz joined the Los Angeles Galaxy soccer team in the United States, and Guatemalan fans continue to follow his career.

Sights to See

ANTIGUA Antigua, often considered the people's capital, has been declared a United Nations Educational, Scientific, and Cultural Organization (UNESCO) World Heritage site because of its fine examples of colonial Spanish architecture. One impressive site is the Palace of the Captains General, which was the finest building in Guatemala when it was built in 1773.

CHICHICASTENANGO This town is the best one to visit to see an authentic market day. Twice a week, tourists and locals alike buy traditional woven goods, crafts, and food at the market. During Chichicastenango's annual three-day celebration of Saint Thomas, the town's patron saint, villagers wear their native dress and join parades through the streets.

DULCE RIVER This picturesque river offers many tourist attractions. The town of Lívingston, located at the point where the Dulce enters the Caribbean Sea, is a thriving Garífuna village. In addition, scenic boat rides travel up the river through the Dulce River canyon, bounded by high limestone walls, to enter Lake Izabal, Guatemala's largest lake.

GUATEMALA CITY As the national capital, Guatemala City is the site of important museums, including the National Museum of Archeology and Ethnology in Parque la Aurora (Aurora Park). This museum houses Mayan artifacts, models of Guatemalan cities and scenes of Mayan city life, and examples of different villages' traditional dress. Also located in Aurora Park is the National Zoo, home to many rain forest animals such as spider monkeys, macaws, jaguars, and tropical snakes.

LAKE AMATITLÁN This lake is a popular recreational area. Its surroundings include the United Nations Park, which has models of Guatemalan sights including the pyramids of Tikal, a typical highlands village, and a Spanish colonial plaza. The Parque Recreativo de Amatitlán has swimming pools, a playground, and boat rides. Unfortunately, the lake also has serious pollution problems.

LAKE ATITLÁN Said by many people to be the most beautiful lake in the world, this lake is circled by three spectacular volcanoes: Atitlán, Toliman, and San Pedro. Although it is a busy center for water sports and vacationers, the lake is also home to the extremely rare poc bird.

TIKAL NATIONAL PARK Set in the tropical lowlands of the Maya Biosphere, this park showcases ruins of some of the largest tiered pyramids of the Mayan civilization, including the Templo del Gran Jaguar. Glyphs etched on many of the structures help scholars search for clues about the Mayan culture. Set aside as a national park in 1955 by the government, Tikal National Park remains one of the best-preserved historic sites in Guatemala.

colonialism: a system of government in which a foreign country rules a dependent country

Communism: a political, social, and economic system based on the idea of common, rather than private, property. In a Communist system, the government controls land, resources, industry, and money, and distributes them among its citizens.

dictator: a ruler with absolute power over the government, who may use extreme or violent methods to hold onto control

gross domestic product (GDP): the total value of all the goods and services produced within the boundaries of a country over a certain length of time (usually one year). GDP does not take into account whether the producers are citizens of the country, so some of the GDP may actually be headed out of the country.

junta: a group of people, usually military leaders, who have seized power. In Spanish, *junta* means "council" or "committee."

left wing: a label often given to a person or political party that favors very liberal (generally reformist) social, economic, and political views. In Guatemala these views include redistributing wealth and land to the poor, and removing the traditional privileges of the military, the wealthy, and the church.

military coup: a rapid strike led by the military to overthrow and take control of a government

rain forest: a large forest of trees in a tropical area where the temperature rarely goes above 93°F (34°C) or below 68°F (20°C). Rain forests get more than 80 inches (203 cm) of rain annually.

right wing: a label often given to a person or political party having very conservative views, which are based on their social, economic, and political traditions and expectations. In Guatemala right-wing views have included strict government control over the people and the protection of the special status or privileges of the military, the wealthy, or the church.

standard of living: a measure of economic well-being. Economists use various factors to calculate standard of living. They might, for example, determine the percentage of an individual's annual income that he or she must use to buy adequate food for one year. By considering these kinds of statistics, economists can determine the level of comfortable living that an individual can reach.

traje: traditional Mayan dress, which varies in design and color from village to village. The main element of the traje for women is a loose-fitting top known as the huipil. Many Mayan men wear rodilleras, woolen garments similar to small blankets and worn wrapped around the waist.

Bernhardson, Wayne. *Moon Handbooks: Guatemala.* Emoryville, CA: Avalon Travel Publishing, 2001.
This guide offers straightforward, travel information on modern Guatemala, as well as good historical summaries and travel advice.

Central Intelligence Agency. *The World Fact Book—Guatemala.* 2002.
<http://www.odci.gov/cia/publications/factbook/geos/gt.html> (December 1, 2003).
This site, compiled by the CIA, presents annual profiles of foreign countries, including Guatemala.

Columbia University Press. "Guatemala." *Columbia Encyclopedia.* 2003.
<http://www.encyclopedia.com/html/G/Guatemal.asp> (December 1, 2003).
This website is a quick source for general information on Guatemala's people, land, history, and government.

DK Compact World Atlas. New York: Dorling Kindersley Publishing, Inc., 2001.
This world atlas includes a map of Guatemala, depicts its flag, and provides a quick Fact File with basic information about the country and its people.

EntreMundos. N.d.
<http://www.entremundos.org> (December 1, 2003).
This newspaper archive contains a wealth of articles on Guatemala, as well as other Latin American countries

Foreign Area Studies, the American University. *Guatemala: A Country Study.* Ed. Richard F. Nyrop. Washington, D.C.: U.S. Government Printing Office, 1983.
This volume in the U.S. government's Area Handbook series offers a wealth of information on Guatemalan history and culture.

Gorry, Conner. *Guatemala.* Lonely Planet Publications, 2001.
This travel guide provides a survey of Guatemalan geography, history, and culture, as well as detailed information on the country's many things to see and do.

Guatemalan Development Foundation. *Guatemala Newswatch.* N.d.
<http://www.quetzalnet.com/newswatch> (December 1, 2003).
This site is an excellent source for current information on important Guatemalan issues.

Institute for Global Communications. *Information Services: Latin America.* 2001.
<http://isla.igc.org/Features/Guatemala/guate1.html> (August 27, 2003).
Check this reliable source for Guatemalan issues of recent world coverage.

Lahmeyer, Jan. "Guatemala: Historical Demographical Data of the Whole Country." *Population Statistics.* 2002.
<http://www.library.uu.nl/wesp/populstat/Americas/guatemac.htm> (December 1, 2002).
This source provides information on the Guatemalan population, including many useful statistics.

Latimer Clarke Corporation. "Guatemala." *Countries A to Z.* **N.d.**
<http://www.atlapedia.com/online/countries/guatemal.htm> (December 1, 2003).
This site is a good, quick reference on Guatemala and other nations of the world.

"Maya Biosphere Reserve." *Guatemala Categoris.* **N.d.**
<http://www.dirla.com/guatemala2_4.htm> (December 1, 2002).
Information on current and past issues related to the protected Maya Biosphere Reserve and other protected areas in Guatemala is provided on this site.

Reuters Foundation. "Guatemala." *AlertNet.* **2001.**
<http://www.alertnet.org/thefacts/countryprofiles/216111.htm> (December 1, 2003).
This website provides a quick description of Guatemala, along with other nations.

Shea, Maureen E. *Culture and Customs of Guatemala.* **Westport, CT: Greenwood Press, 2001.**
This text offers good information on Guatemala, especially on how its history is shaped by cultural differences between native and ladino peoples.

United Nations Office on Drugs and Crime. "Guatemala." *UNDCP Region Office Mexico: Country Information.* **2003.**
<http://www.undcp.org/mexico/country_information_guatemala_mexico.html> (December 1, 2003).
Check this site for a profile of Guatemala from the perspective of the United Nations.

U.S. Department of Energy, Energy Information Administration. *Regional Indicators: Central America.* **August 2002.**
<http://www.eia.doe.gov/emeu/cabs/guatemal.html> (December 1, 2003).
This is an excellent site for information on Guatemala's energy sources and usage. It also has good links to other government websites.

U.S. Department of State. *Guatemala: Country Reports on Human Rights Practices.* **March 4, 2002.**
<http://www.state.gov/g/drl/rls/hrrpt/2001/wha/8344.htm> (December 1, 2003).
This site provides information gathered by the U.S. State Department on Guatemala's human-rights issues.

U.S. Department of State, Bureau of Western Hemisphere Affairs. *Background Note: Guatemala.* **May 2002.**
<http://www.state.gov/r/pa/ei/bgn/2045pf.htm> (December 1, 2003).
The U.S. State Department provides excellent profiles of countries in the Western Hemisphere. Find summaries of Guatemala's history, current |political issues, relations with other countries, and business and travel information.

Asturias, Miguel Angel. *The Mirror of Lida Sal: Tales Based on Mayan Myths and Guatemalan Legends.* Trans. Gilbert Alter-Gilbert. Pittsburgh, PA: Latin American Literary Review Press, 1997.
This collection of stories by Nobel Prize-winning author Asturias brings ancient tales to life, while also discussing the challenges facing modern Guatemala.

CARE. *Virtual Field Trip: Guatemala.*
<http://www.careusa.org/vft/guatemala>
Take a trip to Guatemala with volunteers from CARE, an international humanitarian group. You'll get a feel for the country through journal entries, postcards, and more.

Castañeda, Omar S. *Among the Volcanoes.* New York: Lodestar Books, 1991.
This young-adult novel tells the story of Isabel, a teenaged Guatemalan dealing with the challenges of growing up.

Day, Nancy. *Your Travel Guide to Ancient Mayan Civilization.* Minneapolis: Runestone Press, 2001.
Take a trip back in time to visit life among the ancient Maya.

Haynes, Tricia. *Guatemala.* Philadelphia, PA: Chelsea House, 1999.
This book provides an overview of Guatemala's geography, history, and society.

Menchú, Rigoberta. *I, Rigoberta Menchú: An Indian Woman in Guatemala.* London: Verso Books, 1987.
Although there has been controversy about the accuracy of some of its details, this Mayan woman's memoir of the human suffering that occurred during the civil war remains widely read.

Montejo, Victor. *The Bird Who Cleans the World and Other Mayan Fables.* Willimantic, CT: Curbstone Press, 1991.
This collection of folktales and myths offers a colorful glimpse of Mayan culture.

Nature Conservancy. *Guatemala Program.*
<http://www.nature.org/wherewework/centralamerica/guatemala/>
Get information here on Guatemalan plants, wildlife, and the Nature Conservancy's efforts to protect biodiversity.

O'Dell, Scott. *The Captive.* Boston: Houghton Mifflin, 1979.
This young-adult novel describes the arrival of the Spanish in the Americas and their enslavement of the Maya.

The Rough Guide: Guatemala. London: Rough Guides, 2002.
In addition to travel tips, this guide offers colorful pictures and historical, cultural, and geographical information on Guatemala.

Schlesinger, Stephen C., et al. *Bitter Fruit: The Story of the American Coup in Guatemala.* Cambridge: Harvard University Press, 1999.
This book provides a case study of CIA involvement in the 1954 overthrow of Guatemala's liberal government and the reinstitution of the military dictatorship that led to civil war.

Further Reading and Websites

Travellog.com. *Latin America Cybertravel: Welcome to Guatemala.*
<http://www.travellog.com/guatemala/index.html>
This site offers a wide range of information on Guatemala, including great pictures of local snakes and salamanders.

United States Geological Survey. *Guatemala Volcanoes and Volcanics.*
<http://vulcan.wr.usgs.gov/Volcanoes/Guatemala/
description_guatemala_volcanoes.html>
This is a scientific but highly readable description of Guatemala's volcanoes and a chronicle of their activity.

United States Geological Survey. *Ring of Fire.*
<http://pubs.usgs.gov/publications/text/fire.html>
This site offers a clear explanation of the geological phenomenon of the Pacific Ocean's wide loop of volcanoes.

vgsbooks.com
<http://www.vgsbooks.com>
Visit vgsbooks.com, the home page of the Visual Geography Series®. You can get linked to all sorts of useful on-line information, including geographical, historical, demographic, cultural, and economic websites. The vgsbooks.com site is a great resource for late-breaking news and statistics.

Captions for photos appearing on cover and chapter openers:

Cover: The Temple of the Great Jaguar at Tikal was built around A.D. 700. The 145-foot (44-m) monument covers the tomb of ancient Mayan ruler Ha Sawa Chaan-K'awil (formerly known as Ah Cacau). His burial chamber contained a wealth of information about Mayan culture, including stingray spines that were used for religious bloodletting practices.

pp. 4–5 The outdoor market in Chichicastenango is one of the largest in Guatemala.

pp. 8–9 Surrounded by lush forest, Lake Izabal is Guatemala's largest freshwater lake. It is 228 square miles (591 sq. km) in area and in some places 50 feet (15 m) deep.

pp. 20–21 The stairways of the North Acropolis temple complex descend to the central Great Plaza *(far right)* at Tikal. The plaza has not always been grassy. It was paved with plaster four times between 150 B.C. and A.D. 700.

pp. 38–39 Maya, wearing traditional clothing, watch a religious procession pass along a street in Antigua.

pp. 46–47 A Guatemalan family looks over a street vendor's colorful holiday merchandise.

Photo Acknowledgments
The images in this book are used with the permission of: © Jan P. Snedigar, pp. 4–5, 19 (both), 20–21; © Digital Cartographics, pp. 6, 10; © Reuters NewMedia Inc./CORBIS, pp. 7, 35, 36, 57; © Trip/A. Gasson, pp. 8–9; © Robert Fried Photography/www.robertfriedphotography.com, pp. 13, 24; © Geoff Scott, p. 14; © Kennan Ward/CORBIS, p. 15; © Michael & Patricia Fogden/CORBIS, p. 17; © Trip/D. Hoey, p. 18; © Archivo Iconografico, S.A./CORBIS, p. 23; The Art Archive/Queretaro Musem Mexico/Dagli Orti, p. 26; © Brown Brothers, p. 28; © Bettmann/CORBIS p. 31; © Carl & Ann Purcell/CORBIS, p. 32; © Anita Brosius-Scott, pp. 38–39, 40, 41, 46–47, 49, 50, 51, 52, 53, 54, 60, 63, 64; © Cory Langley, p. 44; The Art Archive/Museo de America Madrid/Dagli Orti, p. 55; © John Tinning; Frank Lane Picture Agency/CORBIS. p. 61; © Todd Strand/Independent Picture Service, p. 68; Laura Westlund, p. 69.

Cover: © Trip/T. Bognar. Back cover photo: NASA.